The office of Overseers©

Biblical Church leadership

CHRISTOPHER E. HOWE

RIGHTLY DIVIDING THE WORD OF TRUTH

II TIMOTHY 2:15 "STUDY TO SHEW THYSELF APPROVED UNTO GOD, A WORKMAN THAT NEEDETH NOT TO BE ASHAMED, RIGHTLY

DIVIDING THE WORD OF
TRUTH."

The office of

Overseers©

Biblical Church leadership

Written by: Christopher E. Howe

This book is dedicated to my Son Jordan Howe who because of his journey to biblical truth was the inspiration in me writing this book.

All scripture references are from the King James Version of the bible. The scripture references are bold, italicized, or underlined for emphasis and does not indicate a change in text

Index

Introduction... 4

Overseers.. 6

Apostles..................................... 11

Prophets........................... 21

Evangelists......................... 27

Pastors.............................. 38

Bishops...............................

..........59

Deacons............................

.........76

Elders...............................

..........86

Timothy and
Titus..........................94

Priests...............................

.........99

Conclusion........................

.........103

Introduction

Over the past couple years, I have started a journey to have Gods best on my life. I am not interested in his mediocre blessings I want his absolute best.

As a Pastor it has become a passion of mine to apply what the bible says and take God at his word. For me to get that best from God I must put my best into God. (Draw nigh to God, he will draw nigh to you... James 4:8)

This has led me to the reality that I MUST seek HIM with my whole heart and to rightly divide the word of truth.

There are a lot of things in the bible that bring controversy and divisions in the church. When it is all said and done the reasons for these divisions are people have stopped believing the bible for what it says. People throughout the years have spent so much time trying to figure out what the bible is saying, instead of just taking it at face value. If God wanted us to waste time trying to figure out what he was trying to say he would not have allowed us to have a bible for what it says. We need to make sure we have a solid foundation.

As I commit to making the bible my ABSOLUTE foundation, I must take it for what it says in the English language. I believe without apology that the Bible is the inspired word of God without error or contradiction. (II Timothy 3:16-17)

This foundation for me is the Holy Bible King James Version. I believe Psalms 12:6-7 that God preserved his word in a perfect form as he said he would without error in the English language. And since God has preserved it, we need to rightly divide this Truth. There will be some parts of this book that having a different translation will lead you in a different direction.

For many years I have heard it taught that a Pastor has had to meet the requirements that are laid out in Timothy and Titus and that a church must give that Pastor the authority to be a pastor.

At the same time, I read in the Bible that God puts Pastors into the ministry and that Bishops are appointed if a man desires. It will be necessary to discuss ALL ministerial positions listed in the Bible starting with Apostles and going down from there.

Then we have all the qualifications of those in the office of Bishops and Deacons and how most (not all) Christians or church leaders pick and choose which of those 17 requirements they are going to hold over that Person and which ones they are ok with

It is crucial that we manage God's business and the church that Jesus Christ himself is the head of, as he gave his life for it. The Bible tells us "Moreover it is required in stewards that a man be found faithful"
 I Cor. 4:2

This book is for my own personal knowledge to dive into what I have discovered from the bible and to rightly divide that truth regardless of popular opinion or opposition I will receive. (My only objective to Rightly Divide the word of truth)
II Tim. 2:15

I only ask that those reading this will take an honest effort to read what I am writing and if there is a contradicting belief that you prove to me through the bible not through man's opinions where I am wrong.

As a Pastor I am responsible to God for what I teach and preach and when I stand before him all I want to hear is well done thou good and faithful servant.

This book will cover a lot of issues and will have a lot of biblical references to it as well. We will also need to look at the life of Timothy and Titus as their roles in the office of an overseer are just as crucial as Pastors and Deacons. Timothy and Titus are known as the pastoral epistles. These epistles deal with how an overseer should conduct himself in ministry and the sheep should conduct themselves in the church as well.

God designed all things to be done decently and in order (I Cor. 14:40) God designed a leadership role in the local church and has placed responsibilities and accountabilities on those roles as well. It is crucial we understand these roles as God established to get his very best in our lives and ministries. Seek God through prayer and ask the Holy Spirit to open your heart of understanding to get that Gold nugget out of this book.

1. <u>OVERSEERS</u>

As we travel down the road of this study it is crucial, we understand the meanings that people use to describe what they or the modern-day church use to associate various roles in church leadership. This is a study on church leadership based on what the bible says. It is not to cause dissention among believers it is just to rightly divide the word of Truth. There will be those that will disagree with the material that is brough up in this book, and that is ok, however if your heart is set on truly understanding the bible for what it says, it is important that you consider without bias this material.

The Pastor is the head of the church and however he runs the church as long as it is in line with the bible is between, he and God. God has granted the Pastor of a church certain liberties. God does not care if one Pastor passes an offering plate, or if one uses an offering box in the back of the building. God does not care if one church uses only hymns, or if one uses a mixture of praise and worship, and hymns. These are some of the liberties that are given to the Pastor as the head of the church.

As I used the phrase travel down the road. I implore you to look at the word overseers as a main road in a local neighborhood with many smaller roads coming off the main road and all the smaller roads have a cul de sac at the end. This being said the smaller roads lead back to the main road of being overseers.

 In the bible we are all overseers. Anyone who is responsible for other people, or others property, or others business is an overseer

I have been taught that a Bishop and Pastor are the same because in the definition they are both overseers. In other versions they use they replace the word Bishop with the word overseer. We will get to each individual position as set up in the bible as this book goes on

I have looked up the definition for overseers in the dictionary, and a Greek dictionary to find that both of them say the same thing.

An overseer simply defined is: *a **person who watches and directs the work of other people in order to be sure that job is done correctly, and one who manages others business or property...***

It has been said among the modern-day church that two positions are the same because one word is the same in their definition. For example the main point of study in this book, that Pastors and Bishops are both are overseers; therefore they must be the same position. Using the definition of an overseer, we must conclude that the nursery director is also a Pastor in a church as she is an overseer and therefore must meet the same qualifications of an overseer, Pastor, deacon to be able to serve in the nursery. We know from reading the bible that this would be absurd so again we must rightly divide the word of truth.

I reached out to two people before starting this book, as I have been working and praying on it for years. The three people I reached out to were my Father whom I believe is a bible scholar, also my biggest critic, and my biggest mentor. The second person I reached out to was my son as his is on his own journey to draw nigh to God. My son and I are both in church seeking God and living for him. Our church leadership structures are very different, his is a board of elders led church and mine is a Pastor led church. I was taught and raised in a Pastor led church and that the church has two basic leadership positions the Pastor and the deacons. I have chosen to not rely on my upbringing and training but to go to the bible and only to the bible to find the truth. We will show in this book that there are actually three biblical positions for church leadership, but one of them has been combined with another over the years. For the churches that use an elder board to run the church, I am not saying that it is a sin to do so or that they are necessarily wrong. Almost all church denominations today are elder led churches, there are some of these churches that are truly seeking God and reaching lost souls for

Jesus Christ. We will establish the role, and responsibilities that God has placed on each office of an overseer along with the accountability that comes with that position.

I wanted to get other opinions and comments to match up with the bible. As I understand this is a very difficult subject. But at the end I just decided that if we are going to use the bible as our foundation, and we know that the bible is spiritually discerned through the work of the Holy Spirit, then we will use only prayer and the bible for our information. This will be almost as difficult as my next book[1] however difficult or not, we must go down these roads

As we will learn in this book that all people talked about in spreading the word of God are overseers, each one had different responsibilities, different people to oversee and different accountabilities to God. We will get into each individual position such as Apostle, Prophet, Evangelist, Pastor and teacher, Bishop, Deacon. We will also study into Timothy and Titus as their roles in this.

---

[1] See the Authors work: The Biblical Family: From Beginning to Blended

God has called and ordained some and then he has allowed those he called and ordained to appoint others to help with the ministry.

Ministry can get very overwhelming at times and to maintain being able to minister to everyone a Pastor must have others to help.

As the bible says, the body is one but many members so are we in Christ and in Christ also in the local church. The Pastor is the head of the church and responsible to God as we will see in chapter four, and those he appoints to help are those of the same church but with different responsibilities to ensure the whole body gets what it needs and ALL are overseers.

1 Corinthians 12:14-17 For the body is not one member, but many. If the foot shall say, Because I am not the hand, I am not of the body; is it therefore not of the body? And if the ear shall say, Because I am not the eye, I am not of the body; is it therefore not of the body? If the whole body were an eye, where were the hearing? If the whole were hearing, where were the smelling?

As we study the different roles of overseers, and the differences between God called, and man appointed positions, this will help us, especially in understanding Biblical church leadership, and to encourage those who are God called, though not perfect people to explore and move toward what God has called them to do.

One other area for me that had been sort of contradictory from what I have been taught to what I have been studying in the bible is if a person is God called and there is fruit in his life why then does the church have to put its authority to either say yes or no to that person? It is good to have witness to the call of God on ones life, but those witness should not take away the calling God put on a mans life to preach, by having to give him permission or not, for the work of the ministry. That man is accountable to God

Churches says a Pastor or Deacon is ordained or licensed to preach by giving them permission to do so. If a church issues a license it can also revoke a license. I have not found in the bible anywhere where a Man of God had to get permission form a church to preach the Gospel. I absolutely disagree with this process. What arrogance the church has to veto a God called Pastor to preach the Gospel just because that Pastor might not be the best spokesmen, or eloquent in speech, or maybe he doesn't always wear a coat and tie. The bible is very clear that God calls Pastors and that if that Pastor has evidence (fruit) of God working in their lives then the church is to put their hand of blessing (ordaining) that person. I am only talking about the God called roles as we will see in the coming chapters.

Ephesians 4:11 And he gave some, apostles; and some, prophets; and some, evangelists; and some, pastors and teachers;

I believe that if a church ordains a minister of any kind, or a Deacon, it should be a conferring ordination not a permission giving ordination. In other words, the church needs to say yes we have seen the fruits of his labor and we believe that call is real and he is seeking the God of Heaven and yes we are going to confer this and lay hands of prayer on him.

God calls and ordains the saved, that we should go and bring forth fruit. God gives permission, not man and this whole idea of licensing a Pastor in my opinion is the most absurd thing I have ever heard. I hope I have not made anyone mad but with a subject like this I most likely will do so.

John 15:16 Ye have not chosen me, but I have chosen you, and ordained you, that ye should go and bring forth fruit, and that your fruit should remain: that whatsoever ye shall ask of the Father in my name, he may give it you.

As we see, everyone is an overseer, even the lay person in the Church as they are to oversee their finances, children, family, etc. that God has given them. The Bible says we are to be good stewards of what God has given us (I Cor. 4:2)

Since we are ALL overseers, we all have the one same purpose, that is to spread the Gospel. That is our primary and only mission. Tell people about Jesus. Everything else is secondary

Ye have not chosen me, but I have chosen you, and ordained you, that ye should go and bring forth fruit God Calls people, people do not call God. God has chosen each and everyone of us for a special purpose. He has called some to preach, he has called some to clean toilets, he has called some to minister to the homeless, but he has called us not us calling him. This will be very important to understand as we move forward in this book. When we get to the chapters on Bishops, and Deacons we will discover that the office of a Bishop and Deacon are chosen by man, where in the chapter on Pastors that office[2] is a God called office and that mans approval is not needed.

____

[2] The bible does not use the word office to describe a Pastor, However for the sake of this book we will refere to it as such

2.
Apostles

Ephesians 4:11   And he gave some, apostles;...

As we continue down this road of Overseers, we come to the side road of Apostles. I have been diligently seeking God on how to identify each position of an overseer or as the bible uses the word "office" I will use office from here on out.

The Lord has led me to ask 5 questions of each office as we will be discussing all of them in this study. The questions are:

1. How is this office called,
   by God, or Appointed by
   man?
2. What are the
   Qualifications of this
   office?
3. What is the responsibility
   of this office?
4. Who was their ministry
   to?
5. Is this office still around
   in today's evangelical
   church?

There must be some basic structure to this study, so I don't go rambling on and on. The first office the Bible talks about in Ephesians 4:11 are Apostles so as we study on this, we will need to go to Acts 1:1-8 to get started

Acts 1:1-8 The former treatise have I made, O Theophilus, of all that Jesus began both to do and teach, Until the day in which he was taken up, after that he through the Holy Ghost had given commandments unto the apostles whom he had chosen: To whom also he shewed himself alive after his passion by many infallible proofs, being seen of them forty days, and speaking of the things pertaining to the kingdom of God: And, being assembled together with them, commanded them that they should not depart from Jerusalem, but wait for the promise of the Father, which, saith he, ye have heard of me. For John truly baptized with water; but ye shall be baptized with the Holy Ghost not many days hence. When they therefore were come together, they asked of him, saying, Lord, wilt thou at this time restore again the kingdom to Israel? And he said unto them, It is not for you to know the times or the seasons, which the Father hath put in his own power. But ye shall receive power, after that the Holy Ghost is come upon you: and ye shall be witnesses unto me both in Jerusalem, and in all Judaea, and in Samaria, and unto the uttermost part of the earth.

The former treatise have I made, O Theophilus, of all that Jesus began both to do and teach, *Until the day in which he was taken up, after that he through the Holy Ghost had given commandments unto the apostles whom he had chosen:*

We see in verse 2 the answer to the first Question, the Apostles are chosen by Jesus. As I will be making clear in this book there are two different offices in the bible. One is God called and the second is man appointed.

God called offices have a very high responsibility and honor to them. There is also a very sever consequence to those who disobey Gods call, we can look at Jonah for that one. I believe also that if a person who is in a God called office starts to divert from the bible and gets involved in sin and lives that way that there are very severe consequences for that as well as we will study in the chapter on Pastors and talking about the Watchman in Ezekiel 33.

To whom also he shewed himself alive after his passion by many infallible proofs, being seen of them forty days, and speaking of the things pertaining to the kingdom of God

We see in verse three that not only did an Apostle have to be chosen but they also had to have seen Jesus. Which leads us to the second Question: What are the qualifications for this office?

We know from verse three that one of the Qualifications was that they had to have seen Jesus, another Qualification is that they Had to of course be saved, as verse five tells us that they were to be Baptized with the Holy Ghost…

We know that when a lost sinner comes to Jesus and accepts him as their personal Savior that he immediately receives the Holy Spirit in his life and is sealed to the day of redemption (Eph. 4:30) This Baptizing of the Holy Ghost is a phrase I hear from time to time in relation to people using it to claim they can speak in tongues and do healings.

It is my conviction that speaking in tongues was a sign that God gave to those in the Apostolic age to prove to the common person that the Apostles had seen Jesus and that the message they were preaching was true and accurate. I do not believe that speaking in tongues or faith healings is a gift that has been give past the Apostolic age as God has preserved his complete word in a perfect form to us today. When speaking in tongues was used there were always interpreters, and everyone heard what was being said in their own language. It is also my conviction that we are not to ask or seek for a sign as signs are recorded in biblical history, from eyewitness testimony, but that we are to believe in Christ, and the Word of God on complete and unwavering faith. This kind of faith builds convictions, and these convictions lead to truth, even truth in martyrdom.

And they were all filled with the Holy Ghost, and began to speak with other tongues as the Spirit gave them utterance.

We must remember that the Apostles also had to usher in Faith to a lost and dying world. All that mankind had up to this point was Old Testament writings and the word of a man who "claimed" to be the Son of God. It was not until Jesus was resurrected from the grave that his "claim" became reality.

The Holy Spirit had to give the Apostles some kind of power and authority to proclaim the resurrection and saving power of Jesus Christ. The Apostles were eyewitnesses to Jesus' resurrection and ascension to the Father.

Even in a court of law eyewitness testimony is proof that something did or did not happen. So, we see here that the message of the Apostles was valid. As the Apostles had to also usher in faith, them speaking in Tongues, doing healings, casting out demons was all proof that they had truly seen Jesus and the message of the cross was truth.

The message of the cross also backed up John the Baptist message and the message of all the Old Testament prophets as well. The message in the Old Testament tells of a future coming Savior to redeem his chosen people. (Chosen people being those who have accepted Christ as their Savior)

So, we have answered from the bible the first two questions the Apostles were God called, through Jesus the Son of God. The Qualifications were that they had to have physically seen Jesus, they had to be saved, and they had received the gift of tongues and healing as proof of their message.

We have today in our modern churches people who call themselves Apostles and based on the bible we have to discredit that title as there were only twelve Apostles who saw Jesus directly.

The third Question to be asked of the office of an Apostle is "What is the responsibility of this office?" for the answer to this Question we must now direct our attention to Matthew 28:18-20 "The Great commission"

Matthew 28: 18-20 And Jesus came and spoke unto them saying All power is given unto me in Heaven and in earth. Go ye therefore, and teach all nations, baptizing them in the name of the Father, and of the Son, and of the Holy Ghost: Teaching them to observe all things whatsoever I have commanded you: and, lo, I am with you always, even unto the end of the world

Acts 1:8 But ye shall receive power, after that the Holy Ghost is come upon you and ye shall be witnesses unto me both in Jerusalem, and in Judaea, and in Samaria, and unto the uttermost part of the earth.

I included Acts in there as well, not only to verify the power of the Apostles talked about already, but to also show the responsibility of the of the Apostles. This verse and the great commission will be used again to show who their ministry was to, to answer question four when we get to that

The Great commission is for all believers but was started with the Apostles. If we break down

Matthew 28:19-20 we can sum it up in four words which we will use to describe the responsibilities of the Apostles. These four words are Go, Tell, Baptize, Teach.

The first of these words is the word GO. Every Christian especially any Christian in an office of an overseer MUST obey. Without obedience God cannot use you. With delayed obedience God cannot use you. God did not call you to go when you have the money, or when your kids have graduated from school, or when you have a job. He had called you to go NOW.

The Apostles had to learn these lessons in obedience before they were Apostles as Jesus had to teach them to deny themselves, to leave all they had or knew, and to follow him unconditionally, and trusting Him to provide for their needs

We in the modern-day church have lost this area of faith in our lives. We are almost to the point of refusing to do anything God has asked us to do unless we know the outcome, or to have all our ducks in a row I can tell you from personal experience with faith if you wait to go you most likely will never go. Stepping out in faith a lot of times makes you look like a fool to the world, just ask Noah.

You will find that by going on faith, that most well-meaning almost bible believing Christians will be your biggest resistance in going. I do not mean to offend anyone but if you claim to be Bible believing and do not live by faith alone through Christ alone then you do NOT believe all of the bible. A person that does not live by faith only believes the part of the bible that fits their lifestyles.

I am a HUGE supporter of missions. There is one area of missions that I do NOT agree with, and that is the area of deputation. God did not call a Missionary to go to the foreign field only once he has been on deputation for three to five years and has a certain percentage of money coming in before he goes.

Let's look at the examples set in Matthew 10:14, Mark 6:11, and Luke 9:5. In these passages Jesus sent the Disciples to go out and tell people about him. He told them to ONLY take their coat and staff and GO. He said to them who every you get to stay with reside there, tell them about repentance and then when you are done leave.

God would meet their need through the people to whom they stayed with.

Jesus also told them that if they were rejected by the homeowner to shake the dust off their feet and continue. It is absolutely clear in the bible that those who are called by God for whatever service or office of an overseer they are to fulfill that they MUST be willing to go, and to go now not to wait until everything falls into place.

I wonder what would have happened if the Apostles had waited till their families had been all set or till they had earned the money they needed for the call or whatever. They would not have ever taken up their cross and followed HIM. One fact for sure if you keep using excuses, even spiritual excuses the Devil will surly provide them.

Faith, true faith is a lost art in today's church and that my friend is the responsibility of Pastors to lead their churches in faith. Money, status, positions, arguments, and gossip have all taken first place in most church and have put faith on the back burner.

The Apostles clearly were to GO, then they were commanded to tell. What was the message to tell? Salvation was this message. Most people do not like this message. I find that a lot of people will listen out of respect but will directly ignore the actual message. Why is this? Because the Gospel in its Holy Ghost power will tell a sinner that he is a sinner, and the sinner does not want to hear that. We as born-again Christians do not really want to hear that message either. Have you ever heard the pastor preach a message and you got angry with what he was saying, well that was the Holy Ghost convicting you of your sinful ways, or thoughts and you did not want to hear it.

It would be interesting to hear Preachers preach the convicting power of the Holy Ghost from the pulpits, it would definitely clear out a lot of churches but at the same time it would bring back that same power on the church, and once a church starts to get the power of God on it then revival can happen.

On my personal journey to get Gods best in my life I want that Holy Ghost, Devil fighting, soul saving power on my life and the ministry that God has allowed me to lead.

To get that power we MUST do what the Apostles did and tell that soul saving, sin fighting, heart convicting, Holy Ghost salvation message to this lost and dying world.

As Christians we are responsible for living our lives according to the bible and letting people see Jesus in us the hope of Glory (Colossians 1:27)

As a Christian you do not have to be an Apostle, prophet, or even a Pastor to tell someone about Jesus. Just live like you love Him and those opportunities will come to you. You may only ever lead one person to Christ, but what if that one person leads ten thousand people to Christ? All God asks you to do is to be willing to do.

As we see with the Apostles, they were the first ones to usher in the great commission, the third word that they were responsible to spread to the world was Baptism.

This is NOT the same baptism we mentioned earlier as this is the water Baptism to identify with Christ and to show the world that you were once dead to your sins and through Jesus Christ, (John 14:6) you are made alive again as a new person, saved and on your way to glory (II Cor. 5:17)

The people in the times of the Apostles were very confused and believed that the baptism that John the Baptist was all they needed for Salvation, but Baptism does NOT save you. Baptism is NOT necessary for salvation, but it is something that every new believer needs to do to show their renewing with Christ.

Just so we are clear baptism before salvation is just a bath without soap. It cannot not, does not save you in anyway. Baptism must occur after salvation.

The Apostles had to set this straight as well as preform baptisms for all the new converts. There were a lot of people receptive to the saving knowledge of Jesus Christ at that time, the bible says there were added to the church (the body of Christ) daily.

The last word we see in the responsibilities of the Apostles was to teach. They were not only to go, tell, and baptize, they were also to teach. This teaching is the teaching of the bible. In that day the complete bible we have today was not available, so the Apostles had to teach through preaching, writing, and living what Jesus had prepared them for.

There were many, many, false doctrines, twisting of the scriptures that they had, and worshiping of idols during that time. Well as you can see nothing has really changed in that area today as we just have different idols we worship.

Teaching of the doctrines was what got the Apostles in the most trouble. Again, people do NOT want to hear about their sin. People are very comfortable in their sins, and in their hearts, they are ok with judging others for their sins while at the same time overlooking their own sins. You can see that throughout the bible, you can be a witness to that in society, and you may even be guilty of it yourself, I know I have been and still struggle with it today.

There are many New Testament books written by the Apostles all dealing with salvation and doctrine. There is NOTHING in your life that the bible does not have an answer for, search the scriptures for yourself, don't be like the majority and just repeat what you heard the Pastor say in church the few minutes you were paying attention, actually sit down and study it, meditate on it, and learn it and apply it to your life.

This quest of mine for the complete power of God and his absolute best on my life has all come for one verse *Matthew 6:33 But see ye first the Kingdom of God, and His righteousness; and all these things shall be added unto you*. We as individuals MUST make time in our lives to study and to learn the Word of God so we can hide it in our hearts to live for Christ the way he has asked us to.

I tell the people in our church almost every Sunday do you want to keep living your life your way and let it continue to end disastrously or do you want to start living your life Gods way and let in end in victory. I also tell them the more of God you put into your life the less the World will be in your life as God and sin cannot be in the same place at the same time the choice is one hundred percent yours.

One last note before we move to question four of "Who was the office of the Apostles to?" the responsibility of your personal walk with God is your responsibility as the bible says we must ALL give an account to God…(Romans 14:12) what do you want God to say to you when you meet him? For me I know I have messed up badly all I want to hear God say to me is well my son you messed up for a while but after you turned back to me all I can say is well done.

The question now is who was the Apostles ministry to? We must go to Acts 1:8 again and we see that they were sent to "...***Jerusalem, and in all Judaea, and in Samaria, and unto the uttermost part of the earth.***"

We can also see in the Great Commission that they were sent to "...***teach ALL nations...***" ***Matthew 28:19*** unto the end of the world. Their mission was to get the message of Jesus Christ to everyone, everywhere, every time they could.

Since there were only twelve of them to initially cover the whole world there had to be delegation going on. It is a wise thing for those in Christ who are called to do Gods work, to disciple others and then once they have received what they needed to do that work, then to send them out into the world or let them do it where they are at.

The Apostles were not to stay in one place for their ministry. They were to plant churches, send Evangelists, ordain Pastors, teach, and train people in biblical doctrines and then to move on to the next city. There was no time limit on how long they were to stay in one area but once the work was started, they were moved on.

We can see from the Bible that after they had works planted that they kept up with those works. Paul was writing letters to the churches to help them stay on track with biblical doctrine. Remember there were a lot of false doctrines back in that day.

The Apostles had to fight against corrupt governments as well who were trying to suppress the gospel from getting out to the average public. Again, people do not like to hear about their sin. Jesus told his disciples that since the people hated him that they would hate his Disciples also.

It is almost a deterrent for the average lost person to accept Christ as their Savior to know that they will not be liked by others. I used to think that and as true as some of that thought might be, the power of the Gospel outweighs any doubt.

In our church we deal ninety-nine percent with the unchurched crowed. A crowed that has twisted biblical views, horrible experiences in other churches, and just a plain love for their sinful behavior. I used to think this was almost impossible to break through, through the Holy Spirit I have learned that the Word of God does NOT need me to defend it. It can stand for what it says each and every time. My job is to preach what it says and do what it says and let God be God and as we have seen, he is God.

I know there were times the Apostles had these thoughts as well. They are human and face the same doubts as others. It is through these doubts that the Christian must make one of two choices. The first choice is, do I stop what I am doing as it seems there is no hope in sight? (living by sight) or the second choice is do I learn to cling to God especially when there seems to be no light at the end of the tunnel. Do I keep being faithful and keep going and trust him (living by faith)

I don't know what choice you will make; I have faced these choices myself in the ministry God has given me and in making my choice all I could do was remember ***Hebrews 11:6 but without faith it is IMPOSSIBLE to please him: for he that cometh to God MUST believe that he is, and that he is a rewarder of them that diligently seek him.*** *(Capitals added for emphasis)*
The Apostles had to face these choices in their ministries and I for one am very glad they chose the faith road as they ushered in the era of

salvation for all through the one and only Jesus Christ.

The last question for the office of the Apostles is "is this office still around in today's evangelical church?" the answer is simple; NO, it is not.

Remember one of the requirements to be an Apostle was to have physically seen Jesus Christ, and no one today has physically seen Jesus. However, their ministry has carried on over the centuries and through the work of the Apostles by making disciples, their message, Gods word, and the Great Commission are still moving forward.

Apostles are overseers and their particular office does not apply to all overseer offices. This is why I believe it is crucial that we understand each particular office of an overseer, as we have in the modern-day church people that still use the titles of prophets, apostles, bishops, etc.

3.

Prophets

Ephesians 4:11   And he gave some, ...prophets,.......

As we now go back down the road of Overseers, we come to the next side road called Prophet Place. This is where we discuss the prophets in the bible answering the same 5 questions as we will for all overseer offices.

As this study is continuing, I am seeing that the churches in today's times are really NOT set up by the examples given in the bible. For most of us it is too late to set up our churches according to the biblical examples. As I am diligently seeking God on this matter our church is still small enough that we can still set it up to this example, with little backlash.

Whatever we decide to do, as this study goes on it will be determined that the Pastor is the head of the church and however, he sets it up is between him and God, and to be honest, it is my belief that God has granted that Pastor, not elder board, the privilege to set up the local church government how he determines to do so.

Now onto the prophets. We hear prophets mentioned all through scripture when I looked it up there were approximately 455 mentions of prophet in the bible. Most of the mentioning of prophets in the New Testament was a reference to old Testament prophets.

As we get into the qualifications of the prophet there really was no need for the prophets once Jesus came on the scene. When Jesus does mention about a prophet in his day, he said we were to know them by their fruits. Knowing people who are Christians or people of God by their fruits is a very critical process which is greatly overlooked in today's church. I hear in other denominations people called Prophets, I mentioned in the last chapter people use the title Apostles also. These again are not rightly dividing the word of truth. As we will see when we get to the chapters on Pastors and elders there are certain qualifications for these offices of overseers. Again, I am not coitizing any person, Pastor, church, or denomination, I am simply saying we have veered from the biblical model set in place. If we want Gods best in our lives, we MUST do life, church, and everything Gods way. (If I do, He will)

The prophets were used by God himself to get his message to people. Prophets were mostly used to bring a sinful person or nation to repentance so healing and restoration could be done. People, because of their sinful nature always seem to go the way of the world. This is a simple process to overcome as stated in ***Galatians 5:16 This I say then, Walk in the Spirit, and ye shall not fulfil the lust of the flesh.***

If we would just keep our hearts and minds focused on God by reading our bibles and praying and seeking God with ALL our hearts, oh the heartache we could avoid. But when things are going ok in our lives or we are on that mountain top we seem to not need God and then we drift back toward the world.

The first of our questions to ask of a prophet is, is this prophet called by God or appointed by man? To answer this question we need to look at *Numbers 12:6-8 and he (God) said, Hear now my words: if there be a prophet among you, I the LORD will make myself known unto him in a vision, and will speak unto him in a dream. my servant Moses is not so, who is faithful in all mine house. with him I will speak mouth to mouth, even apparently, and not in dark speeches; and the similitude of the LORD shall he behold: wherefore then were ye not afraid to speak against my servant Moses?*

There was a lot of meat in those three verses as to how a prophet becomes a prophet. We all know from any reading of the bible that Moses was known and called a prophet throughout the scriptures. He was a man who was faithful to God. Moses did have his issues as like most of us. Moses had that whole murder thing going against him, but God was still able to use him.

I love the passages in Jeremiah where the potter was making a vessel and when he saw that mar in the clay, that instead of throwing away the clay he remade the vessel with the mar and all. It is these mars, these imperfections, these sins that had to be repented of that makes a person usable to God. God cannot use a perfect person.

There is not one mention of a person God used in the bible to get his will accomplished that did not sin and had to repent of that sin to get restored so God could use him. With every sin comes a consequence and sometimes those consequences follow us our entire lives. Even after forgiveness and restorations we still must face these and they can be hindrances to our ministries, but they can be used greatly to understand the deeper love of God in our lives.

and he (God) said, Hear now my words: if there be a prophet among you, I the LORD will make myself known unto him in a vision, and will speak unto him in a dream.

We can see from these verses that a prophet receives his call from God. This is not an appointed position that someone can say ok you are now a prophet and we will ordain you to that.

A prophet had to be called (The LORD would make himself known) or his message would not be true. Remember, the bible was not around back then as it is today, so the word of God had to come from God. We see in these two verses that the word of God came by two different methods. The first method was making himself know in a dream, and then speaking in a vision.

The second method God used to call a person as a prophet was a mouth to mouth method mentioned in verse eight. Mouth to mouth was used a lot in the Old Testament. The prophets had to hear the word of God in an Audible voice, or in a vision and even in some cases an Angle of the LORD had visited so the person who was the Prophet would know that the message they were about to share was from God.

As I stated a couple of times in this book, the bible was not complete and most of the prophets wrote books of the Old Testament to record what God had told them.

The answer to the first question is the prophet HAD to be called by God not man. Since the prophet was called by God, he was responsible directly to God for what he did or did not do. God was accountable for the prophet as the prophet was accountable to God in that he had to obey the call and be on a path to seeking God.

The next question does not have a straight answer by any one verse, but we can still answer it as to the people God did call throughout the bible. This next question is that of "What are the Qualifications of this office?"

As demonstrated, all through scripture God does NOT use men or women who reject him or his word. So, we can say with certainty that God uses those who are trying to serve him. We can also see that there must be obedience as with anything God asks us to do.

We remember the story of the prophet Jonah, how he was called by God to preach a message to a sinful nation and he refused to obey. As a result of his deliberate disobedience to God he had a Whale of an experience which got him to obey.(insert laugh here) One thing we must remember about Jonah was that even though he finally obeyed he did it reluctantly. God still blessed his obedience, but Jonah missed out so much on Gods best for his life because of his reluctance to obey.

As we study the story of Jonah, we should ask ourselves is there something God is wanting me to do and I am disobeying? Is there something I am doing that God has asked me to do but I am doing it reluctantly? There are many, many miserable Christians in this world today who if they would just have faith and do what God is asking them to do and do it with a God like heart what a difference it would make in spreading the gospel

Seeking God, and obedience are seen throughout the scripture as a qualification for God using someone, their attitude also plays a part as we see with Moses. In Numbers 12:3 we see Moses had a very meek personality the bible says it was meeker than all other men. Mariam meek simply defined is: having or showing a quiet and gentle nature: not wanting to fight or argue with other people"

Personality plays a part in Gods call on someone he wants to use. I believe he uses the person with the personality for the particular job he wants for them to do that no other can do. I mean many people God can use as prophets, however he only used one of them to reach Nineveh. He only used one to free the children of Israel from Egyptian bondage.

The third question we ask of all offices of an overseer is "What is the responsibility of this office" In a more simplified term the Prophet was to preach what God said to a certain area where God chose and to do this preaching no matter what popular opinion may have been.

We will see that the results of this preaching produced different results. We see in Nineveh the lost people repented and turned back to God, we see in Sodom the people continued to reject the word of God and destruction was their fate. God does not want anyone to be destroyed we see that in 2 Peter 3:9 that Gods initial intent is that every person come to repentance. Once that repentance has been performed than God can heal II Chronicles 7:14. If a person or nation continues to reject God then there is no choice but destruction. God is God and he needs to be worshiped as such. It's not that people mess up in life it is that rejection. Rejection is a deliberate, thought out rebellion against something. This is the problem of society.

Not all Prophets were to preach repentance only, some were to interpret dreams of future coming kingdoms, as with Daniel, some were to prophesy of future coming events like a redeemer coming to save his people from their sins, as with Isaiah, Some prophesy of the end of time. Whatever the message was, it was the responsibility of that prophet to carry that out.

I think of my hero of the bible other than the Lord Jesus Christ and that is Elijah. He had the power of God on his life as he was able to pray for rain

to stop then to restart again. He had that power
so much that at Gods word he challenged the
false prophets to a showdown to see whose God
was real and who's was not. I love the prayer of
Elijah on Caramel as he told God **At thy word** I
Kings 18:36 Elijah took God at his word in the
face of people who were following the false
prophets. Then at the end when God showed up
then Elijah defeated the prophets and had them
all killed.

God in the Old Testament had those who
practiced evil and rejected him killed. Not only
them but their families, including children and
their cities to be destroyed and burned. This was
done to stop the continued spread of evil. Ever
wonder why we don't see this kind of thing
happening today? It is because we are under the
NEW covenant and part of that new covenant is
that whosoever is not found written in the book
of life is cast into the lake of fire for all eternity.
That will be the end of all evil and rejection.

In this sense we are all prophets telling lost
people about the bible and what it says. It is our
responsibility to spread the Gospel to a lost and
dying world. I cannot emphasize enough how
important it is for us to live like Christ is in us and
not live like we are miserable.

The next two questions are not as hard to answer as basic bible reading can see the answers. The next question is "who was their ministry to" well that one is probably the simplest. All prophets were to a certain people group. Prophets did not travel across the globe to spread the message as did the Apostles. They were chosen for a specific group of people designated by God for a specific reason. They were equipped with what they needed for that specific task at hand and they had to rely totally on God in everything they did

The last question is "is this office still around in today's evangelical church" the answer to that is no. there are no true bible prophets around today.

Remember God had to verbally speak to a prophet either by voice, in a dream AFTER he made himself know to that person, or through a visible appearance of his Angle who was bringing the word to the prophet.

We have the complete word of God in our hands and what God has put in the bible has not, nor will not change. He will not need to speak to someone in person to tell them something that is different from what the bible says. As earlier in some sense we are ALL prophets listening to, and reading the bible to hear the voice of God in scripture

4.

Evangeli
sts

As we now go back down the road of Overseers, we come to the next side road called Evangelists Court. The office of an Evangelist has changed some in the modern-day church. I hope to make a clear understanding of the role the Evangelist played in the bible and the role the Evangelist plays in the church today.

As we start down this road, we must look at scripture and how the original Evangelist came about and what the Bible says or uses as examples for a person to be an Evangelist. We will again look at all five of these questions when considering this office of an overseer.

An Evangelist defined is: ***A writer of any of the four Gospels; A person who evangelizes; specifically: a Protestant minister or layman who preaches at special services,*** it is also defined as: ***a person who seeks to convert others to the Christian faith, especially by public preaching. The writer of one of the four Gospels.*** Don't forget this one: ***A preacher or publisher of the Gospel of Jesus Christ, licensed to preach, but not having charge of a particular church***.

We can see two very distinct similarities in all three of the definitions. The first distinction is that they were to preach the message of Jesus Christ, and they could also be a writer. This makes the Apostles Matthew, Mark, Luke, and John among others, also evangelists.

One thought we have to keep in mind when dealing with offices of overseers is that the higher office can do the work of a lower office. The lower office, however, cannot do the work of the higher office unless the qualifications and conferring are there.

Let's use business as a great example of the higher and lower offices. In a business structure you have employees, and managers. In the manager roles there are many levels. Take a department supervisor, that person manages that department to make sure the shelves are stocked, maybe oversees the one or two employees in that department. That supervisor is responsible for the day to day restocking, cleaning, etc. in that department.

That supervisor reports to a section manager who is over five departments. Each department in that section has a supervisor but one manager oversees the five supervisors. The section manager can stay in one department, and supervisor it, if the supervisor for that department was absent that day. That section manager would then have to do that supervisors job as well as their own until the return of the supervisor. However, if that section manager were out, the department supervisor would not be able to run all five departments and their own, as they have not been trained or met the qualifications of that manager position.

Both management positions are positions of overseers, however the offices they hold have different responsibilities and accountabilities. This is what we see with some of the Apostles also being Evangelists.

Acts 6:1-7 And in those days, when the number of the disciples was multiplied, there arose a murmuring of the Grecians against the Hebrews, because their widows were neglected in the daily ministration. Then the twelve called the multitude of the disciples unto them, and said, It is not reason that we should leave the word of God, and serve tables. Wherefore, brethren, look ye out among you seven men of honest report, full of the Holy Ghost and wisdom, whom we may appoint over this business. But we will give ourselves continually to prayer, and to the ministry of the word. And the saying pleased the whole multitude: and they chose Stephen, a man full of faith and of the Holy Ghost, and Philip, and Prochorus, and Nicanor, and Timon, and Parmenas, and Nicolas a proselyte of Antioch: Whom they set before the apostles: and when they had prayed, they laid their hands on them. And the word of God increased; and the number of the disciples multiplied in Jerusalem greatly; and a great company of the priests were obedient to the faith.

The qualifications for an Evangelist are given to us in Acts 6:1-7 where the Apostles could no longer meet the daily needs of the people under their ministry. They could not stay in the local church for their ministry as they had to fulfill their specific responsibilities as Apostles to get the gospel to the world and to plant and help churches along the way. So, they appointed seven men of good report to oversee the daily ministration of the local church. These seven and their responsibilities were doing the work of Deacons in a church, not the modern-day deacons as we will see in that chapter, but biblical deacons. (please read the chapter on

Deacons before anyone gets mad at that
statement)

In Acts 6 one of the seven men named was
Philip who is not the same as the Apostle Philip.
This Philip one of the seven we see again in
Acts 21:8 and he is called an Evangelist.

*Acts 21:8 And the next day we that were of
Paul's company departed, and came unto
Caesarea: and we entered into the house of
Philip the evangelist, which was one of the
seven; and abode with him*

Philip was one of the seven in Acts 6 and he was
an evangelist as well so now we can go back to
Acts to answer the five questions about this
office. On a side note did you know the word
"evangelist" only appears three times in the
bible? Two of those times it mentions two people
by name, Philip and Timothy

*Acts 6:3 Wherefore, brethern, look ye out
among you seven men of honest report, full
of the Holy Ghost and wisdom, whom we
may appoint over this business.*

The first of the five questions is "how is this
office called, by God, or appointed by man?" to

answer this question we must use the only examples we have of evangelists. The two examples that are identified in the bible are Philip and Timothy, which were both appointed and ordained (conferred) by man. We will discuss Timothy in greater detail in that chapter as well.

Philip was set apart out of a crowd in Acts 6 along with 6 other men. The Bible makes no mention of the other six being an evangelist or not being an evangelist. I am NOT going to speculate on those six, as we will only discuss what we do know.

Timothy was appointed by Paul to stay at Ephesus and to help that church get doctrinally sound and to help them establish their church structure. We see this in the book of I Timothy and in Verse three we see that Paul besought (appointed) Timothy to stay. In II Timothy 4:5 Paul tells Timothy to "do the work of an evangelist"

The second question is "what are the qualifications of this office?" we can start to answer that in Acts 6:3 the first thing that was told of the of the brethren was to find seven men "of honest report"

To have an honest report one must have demonstrated that characteristic to people around them. If you had a huge group of friends that you have grown up with and someone ask you who is the most honest of your friends, you could have a couple of their names run to your first thoughts.

We all have people we know that if there was ever a question of honesty, we would know who in our realms tell the truth and who don't. it may even be that some only lie or mislead occasionally and those names would not come first to your mind. I have had people at my work come to me when they are feeling bad, or something bad has happened in their lives and they need someone to talk to.

If I were to ask you who in your life is Christian or not you would be able to name a name or two right away. This is what it means to have an honest repot. A person must have demonstrated his character trait to those around him. This does not mean that a person must be perfect, just on a consistent basis demonstrate his honesty.

I remember once when my son saved up his money to buy a video game and I took him to go get it. He did not have the money for the newest version but for the version that was two years old. When we got home, he had opened the case and he came and told me that the clerk had put the newest version in the box by mistake. My son was so excited until I told him, let's go back to the store and tell them what happened and get the version we paid for. Imagine the disappointment on his face. So, we went back to the store and told the clerk. The clerk looked very surprised and said well the case for the new version was already opened and he could no longer sell it as the new version, so we were told to keep it.

This is part of an honest report doing the honest thing especially when no one knows the wrong thing was done. It is crucial as Christians that we show this honest report to a lost and dying world.

After looking for men of honest report the next on the list was full of the Holy Ghost and wisdom. There is only one way to be filled with the Holy Ghost, and that is to be walking a life with God. Separating yourself from the world and the sin that is in it. To walk with God, one MUST be daily in the Word, continually in prayer, and determined to walk circumspectly in this world

Most Christians today can't even spend five minutes talking to God and only open their bibles on church days, and even then, it is very scares. Most people, Christians and non-Christians can quote verses from the bible that make them feel good, or that they can use to judge others with. It is the verses that convict our own hearts and souls, the verses that drop us to our knees in repentance that change our lives and draw us closer to God.

I always refer to Matthew 6:33 to seek God FIRST and foremost in every single situation in our lives and he WILL handle it. As one draws closer to God, he draws closer to them we read that in James. As we walk with God, seek him daily, and get the sin out of our lives, we then start to see a glimpse of the grace of God in our lives. We then start to get a taste of the Holy Ghost leading us in our lives. We WILL be known by our fruits.

One can play church or play walking with God only for so long. Galatians 6:7 tells us that God is not mocked and that whatsoever a person sows, that he will reap. This is simply saying that when one is only pretending sooner or later their true walk will be exposed. This is sometimes very hard to tell in a person.

A Pastor will sometimes make a bad choice on who they put in what position based on that persons pretend fruit. When that does happen then the steps to correct that have to be taken.

Not only were these seven to have been filled with the Holy Ghost but they had to be filled with wisdom. The bible tells us in James 1:5 if any of us lack wisdom we should ask God for it as he gives it out. I have found the best way to get wisdom is through prayer, fasting, and searching the bible.

The bible as we stated earlier in this book has the answer for everything in our lives. So let's go to the book of wisdom.

Solomon was the wisest person in the bible. We are told in scripture that no man will ever have the kind of wisdom that Solomon had but God will give us wisdom in the ministry he has for us to do. I may not have wisdom to run a nation, or to settle wars, or even make money in the stock market, but God gives me wisdom as I ask for it in the church he has me in, in the job he has me working, and the family he has given me to lead. Am I perfect at it, ABSOUTLY not but as I continue to seek God and ask him for wisdom, that wisdom comes more and more.

In Acts 6:5 we see one more character trait that the brethren used in choosing the seven and that was faith. we see in this verse they chose Stephen being a man of faith and filled with the Holy Ghost. The bible does not mention that Stephen was an evangelist. I do not believe that all seven were an evangelist just as you may have five men called to preach and three Pastor churches, one becomes a missionary, and the other an evangelist. All are preaching the gospel just in different areas of life.

Faith is something that needs to be seen in a person. It is not an easy task at all to seek after faith. The only true faith is a tested faith. you may agree or disagree but when you are at rock bottom of life, or you are hours away from being homeless, or get a sickness, lose a family member, or numerous life disasters this is when a person's faith is tested.

I have talked to a few people who are, for lack of better words, all arrogant and full of knowledge of the bible and telling others about their sin, but you can tell from their conversations that they have never had their faith tested. There is a certain humbleness in a person whose faith has been tested, tried, and stood the test. You can see the grace of God in their lives. This same faith should be a best practice for appointing a person to any overseer role.

Some people who are seeking God and may not have yet had those tests of true faith can still be appointed to offices as long as they are seeking after God and that evidence is in their lives. By them seeking God they will have people in their lives to help them get through those tests. Any Christian that is serving God according to the word of God will have their faith tested, this is made clear in the bible II Timothy 3:12

The third Questions we ask about this office is "what is the responsibility of this office?" The responsibilities of an evangelist is like most other offices as an overseer and that was to spread the gospel. The evangelist in today's times is not to pastor churches but to go to and from preaching and teaching the bible. This has not always been the case in bible times.

We can see in the bible that evangelist Philip not the Apostle Philip went to meet a man from Ethiopia. This man was a Eunuch and Philip explained to this Ethiopian about what he was reading and then the man got saved and Philip baptized him.

We can also see Acts 6:5 that Philip was to help minister to the needs of the widows and others in this growing congregation. Also, we see in Acts 8:9-13 that Philip was also preaching and rebuking a sorcerer who got saved.

Philip as an evangelist was to preach the gospel, go to others out from the local church, and was to help minister to the needs of the local church in which he was working with.

We can see with Timothy who as an evangelist was to work with churches to help the pastors get the correct doctrines, and to help to ordain elders, to help serve in the local churches. Timothy was commissioned by Paul to go ordain elders in EVERY city. Timothy was not to stay in one church for a long period of time. We will get into detail on Timothy in the chapter called Timothy

The evangelists of this time were to help get churches planted both locally and abroad. Evangelists today go from church to church, city to city, and country to country, and preach in weeklong crusades, preach, and teach where they can. Their number one focus is to get the gospel out and then move on to the next place on the calander.

Today's church has split the role of evangelists. They have taken the church planting part and shifted that to missionaries and keep the travailing part to the evangelists. The missionaries are basically pastors who go to foreign countries and plant one or many churches, however God leads them to do this.

The term Missionary is nowhere in the bible; however, we see that Apostles, and evangelists were both missionaries of their times. Since missionaries are church planters and stay to pastor churches, they must fall under the same qualifications of Pastors which we will study in the next chapter. Missionaries are usually sent out by a local church for the purpose of establishing new churches in other places or countries

Missionaries today I believe most do NOT live by faith but rather by sight. Let me start by saying I love deeply and support missions and getting the gospel to the lost and dying world. What I mean by missionaries living by sight is simply this, the entire process of a missionary going on deputation for 2 to 5 years to raise money for support before they go to the mission field, in my opinion is delayed obedience, and not trusting God to provide the needs. There is no verse in the bible that supports a missionary going on deputation, there are no examples in the bible of one being called to go and they had to get other things done first. It was a call, then a going, with a trusting, and exercising of one's faith. Without FAITH it is IMPOSSIBLE to please God (Hebrews 11:6)

Jesus told the Apostles to GO, tank NOTHING with you, and that God would meet their needs. I can tell you of a faith experience. As I felt the moving of the Lord in my life to move across the country to plant a church, we had left with only a moving truck. I must confess I did wait till I got a job before we moved. I was not sure of the call being from God or from my emotions as a lot of people react on their emotions, as I have for many years.

I asked the Lord to show me where in Colorado he wanted me to move. My wife and I put up maps and started praying for the city in Colorado he wanted us to move to. We had two cities that keep getting on our minds but did not have a hundred percent peace about it. As we kept praying, Colorado Springs kept coming to mind, it was the very first thing we could think of when we prayed about this move. My wife and I made a trip out here for vacation that year to see the city and see if God would confirm that call. We stayed in a hotel that week and it was snowing. We had never been in snow as coming from Florida. So, we made the trip enjoyed the vacation. We felt like this was the place but was not sure of the time as I was serving as a youth director in my church.

I had filled out applications all over Colorado three month prior to the vacation. I told the lord wherever he gave me the job is where we would plant the church. Well wouldn't you know it exactly two weeks to the day we got back from our vacation a company called me. They were opening a new branch and needed truck drivers. The manager asked me if I have ever heard of Colorado Springs, I laughed and told him the story.

That was the living by sight part which I have repented of and have received God's forgiveness for. Here is where the faith part comes in. I had four weeks to start this job in Colorado Springs, I had already been working with my pastor about us moving but we did not know when. After the interview on the computer I made the commitment to go. I told the pastor and started to turn over our youth ministry to someone else. I had to go before my wife could because she was teaching at our church school and the year was six weeks from being over.

I had four weeks to get there with no way to get there and nowhere to stay and no money to pay for the trip. But said go, and I told God if he wants me there, he must pay for it. I resigned from my job in Florida, and two weeks before I was to go to Colorado the Lord provided me a car. I had a small amount of money saved just enough to buy this car. So, God provided me transportation to get there.

Now I needed a place to stay. One week before I was to leave, I found a Christian man on the internet who has a four bedroom house with a room to rent. I called him, he was looking for someone longer term, but I told him I was only going to need it for about six weeks and he just happened to have a six week gap of time before his next long term tenant was to come in.

I made the commitment with taking the room and then moved. I was to start his job but there were complications. We all know the Lord will not let you step out on faith without him testing that faith. I ended up being up here almost five weeks with no paycheck and only the two hundred dollars my wife was making at the church school to support both households. The one in Florida and mine in Colorado. GOD MET EVERY NEED as he said he would.

I believe that any person that God calls to ministry needs to go when he calls them to go, and not wait. Stepping out on faith is a lost art in our churches today. Just sit in any church you will see big buildings, with large debts to pay, pastors won't accept pastorates unless they are making a certain amount of money. This Christian world today lives by sight and not faith. we need more faith.

This is what I mean when talking about missionaries or Evangelists going on deputation to raise support for their ministries. For evangelists going on faith provides many, many, opportunities to get the gospel out. For example, fill your tank with gas, start to evangelize on the streets, in churches, parks, etc. then when you run out of gas trust God to pay that gas money, as you wait for God to provide witness to the people at the gas pumps.

God will provide. As an evangelist's ministry grows churches will take on the evangelist for monthly support and God will use his people to meet his needs. Forget the loans, forget the salaries in ministry, forget the benefits. These are all man provided, let God be God, believe the bible for what it says, trust in the Lord and he SHALL supply ALL you need (Philippians 4:19)

The fourth question we come to is "who was their ministry to?" the ministry of an evangelist is the same as those of Apostles. to go to the world, the utter most parts and preach the gospel. Preach about the saving blood of Jesus Christ. Their ministry is also to their neighbor.

An evangelist when he starts should start where he is called to, then as God leads, go to other areas. It is crucial that an evangelist wait till God moves him verses him making the move to help God. We see in the bible (Acts 8:26) the Angle of the Lord sent Philip to talk to the Ethiopian. Philip did not just go because he felt like it. I can promise you with all certainty that if you live by faith God will make it clear when HE, not you, wants to move you.

My God is big enough to put people where he wants them to use them how he wants them. If you doubt that read your bible. If you don't trust God to meet your needs, and to meet his own needs in your ministry then you have a faith issue.

Evangelists and missionaries like Pastors have to live by faith to get Gods absolute best in their lives and ministries. Ever wonder why the church is dying today? it is because Pastors don't live by faith, some may preach living by faith, but their lives do not reflect it. Here is the reality of living by faith, people especially born-again Christians will persecute you for living by faith. they will tell you not to, that you are foolish, and all sorts of comments. If you know that you know that your call is of God, then Go. remember Noah looked extremely foolish for a hundred and twenty years until that very first raindrop.

The last question is "is this office still around in today's evangelical church?" that answer is yes. I mentioned earlier it has been split into two different offices in today's church the one still being the evangelist, who basically travels and preaches the gospel, then the second office is the missionary who for all practical purposes is a pastor who goes to a foreign field and plants churches.

As the evangelist does not pastor a local church and mainly all he preaches is salvation, the missionary will pastor a local church just his church will be in a different location and he will not just preach salvation but all the bible. He will teach in doctrine, and disciple converts for the cause of Christ.

Not many evangelists today write books or focus much on daily ministrations. They focus on revivals, on getting the word of God out, maybe preaching weeklong camp meetings. It is great for a Pastor to have evangelists come to their churches and preach. When we get to a church that has a building and we can have revivals, we will do it every year with one evangelist and one pastor preaching each night. What a great way to get people to see what is wrong in their lives, for the Holy Spirit to get them to repentance, then all can be restored and Gods power brought back into the church

5.

Pastors

Ephesians 4:11   And he gave some, ...pastors and teachers,.......

As we now go back down the road of Overseers, we come to the next side road called Pastor Place. This is going to be detailed and if you are still with me on this book and have not put it down or called me a heretic, please, ask the Holy Spirit for guidance, wisdom, and discernment before proceeding.

Again, I ask that if you do not agree that you show me from the bible where I am not rightly dividing the word of truth. It is not my intent to offend anyone just to go with what the bible says. This information has been on my heart for years and I must put it to words to help with the studying on this difficult subject.

Everything from this point on will deal with the local church. It will deal with the Pastor being the head of the church and ALL functions of the church should be under the authority of the Pastor as described in the bible. All offices of overseers other than the Pastor, are to be under the Pastor's authority whether that local church has allowed that Pastor that authority or not. We will also show that pastor's responsibility to GOD for how he operates the church Jesus gave his life for. Here we go.

The first question we ask is "how is this office called, by God, or appointed by man?"

Jeremiah 3:15 And I will you Pastors according to mine heart, which shall feed you with knowledge and understanding

Ephesians 4: 11 and He (God) gave some, apostles; and some, prophets; and some, evangelists; and some pastors and teachers;.....parentheses added

It is clear in the bible that a Pastor is called by God and not appointed by man. In Jeremiah we see that God gives pastors after his own heart. And again, in Ephesians we see that God GAVE some pastors and teachers.

Pastors must be called by God. In the modern-day church we have a system set up that anyone who so desires can become a pastor. This is in some part a confusion based on one of the pastoral epistles in I Timothy 3:1 where the verse says that if a man DESIRES the office of a bishop. We will see as we move forward that a Pastor and Bishop are NOT the same office. However we will show that according to the bible that a Pastor and a shepherd are the same.

This confusion has enlisted many years of debate and rejecting from ministry those that GOD has put in place. We will get into the role of a bishop in the next chapter. In the King James Bible, the word Pastor is mentioned 9 times. In most other versions the word pastor is not mentioned, and if it is it is only once. The word bishop as well is ONLY mentioned in the KJV. The words pastor has been changed to shepherd, and the word bishop has been changed to overseer.

Our immediate chapter on pastors we see that a Pastor must be called by God. It is the only office of an overseer that God says that he will provide that person and that that person will be AFTER his own heart.

A pastor must be walking with God to be able to lead Gods church where he needs for it to go. a pastor is also a shepherd, a watchman, a consoler God has given pastors only certain abilities and talents to be able to handle the demands of a pastorate. It is so much more than just preaching on Sunday morning, Sunday night, and Wednesday night. It is a twenty-four-hour, seven day a week job.

For a Pastor to be after Gods own heart he must be walking with God daily. This walk must include, personal prayer, bible study, and fasting to get the power of God on his ministry.

In today's church we have taken the authority that GOD has given a pastor and placed it in the hands of a board of people who do not have that God given authority in Gods own church. We have told God you may have called them, but we must approve them. This is a very unscriptural and dangerous process that has been put into motion.

I have seen people that you can tell by the fruits in their lives that God has called into ministry as a pastor, that a church board has said no to or rejected completely because that person did not meet their highest standards. To that I say hogwash. God have mercy on the people who rejected or still reject Gods man.

The Pastor as he is called and placed by God is equally accountable to God for his walk with God and his leading Gods sheep to the promised land. If that pastor is a false pastor or is not seeking God, God tells us that he will hold the blood of all those he did not warn of their ways on that pastor's head.

God holding a Pastor accountable is far worse than what man could ever do to that person. If a pastor is going astray and teaching and preaching a wrong gospel will the church sometimes suffer along with him? I would say yes. It is in difficulties and stress that we all as Christians learn to get closer to God and let GOD remove that pastor as well. If God is God enough to put a pastor in that office he can surely remove that pastor as well.

The average church has an "elder" board to whom the pastor basically works for. If a pastor is in a church like that and that board vetoes a decision of that pastor or stops that pastor from doing what God has convicted his heart of doing, God will still hold that Pastor accountable, not the board. This is where pastors need to be careful. If they surrender their God given authority to a man-made board, they CANNOT surrender their accountability to that board. See here is the thing, God will never surrender his will to the authority of man.

Matthew 6:24 No man can serve two masters: for either he will hate the one, and love the other; or else he will hold to the one, and despise the other. Ye cannot serve God and mammon. This verse will confirm another point to a Pastor who works for a board and not for God. the bible is very clear that you absolutely, positively, completely, dogmatically cannot serve both God and Man. We have a huge disconnect in the church today when it comes to bible preaching. Pastors want to keep their jobs with the church. Pastors have come to the point that to keep those jobs, and the benefits of those jobs that they will water down the bible as not to offend anyone.

Pastors are holding to the elder boards at the cost of despising what God has told them to do. It is a sad day to see that a lot of those in a Pastor position are there just for the benefits of that job. Most of these are not God called, as God called men will do the job as a ministry trusting God to meet the needs and not man. If a God called man is in a church that can provide for the Pastor that is a very good thing, however it does not need to be the main focus. And see what happens to that Pastor once those benefits are gone.

A pastor will not be able to serve both a board of elders and God at the same time. If a board led church was what God wanted instituted in his church than this verse would be a complete contradiction to scripture. God called Pastors need to preach the word without fear of losing their jobs, because if God has called them it is not a job, but a calling, they may have to work a job to meet some needs, but as a calling God will provide for them.

The pastorate has become more of a career opportunity for people and no longer a calling. Ever wonder why pastors quit the ministry in massive numbers every year? Ever wonder why pastors are committing suicide or "Leaving the faith" as they are doing this day? It is because they were never called to the pastorate by God. They were appointed by a board who did NOT rightly divide the word of truth, and they used the requirements for a man appointed position to qualify of disqualify a Pastor who is God called. They quit when the going got tough. None of the apostles ever quit when the going got tough. No GOD CALLED pastor will ever quit pastoring or take his own life if he is truly seeking God, because he knows that God will make a way.

If you ask anyone in ministry what are the requirements for a pastor, they will quote to you the qualifications listed in Timothy and Titus and say those are the qualifications for a pastor. Well let me challenge you to find in those two books that says anything about having the call of God on their lives. They can't find them because that qualification is NOT in that section. However, it does say that a man, of his own free will, can chose to apply for that office and that it is a good thing.

Once the Call of God is no longer a requirement for a Pastor you then have churches who no longer live by faith or have the power of God on the lives of the people in that church. Without the call of God on a pastor the door is very open for the world to come in and be accepted. If you doubt this just look at the modern-day church. We have denominations now splitting because some want homosexual pastors to be accepted and others do not. this is a result of removing Gods call from the requirements of a pastor. Why has the requirement of Gods call on a Pastor been replaced with "if he desires" the answer is I believe in two parts. Part one is as stated a minute ago we have not rightly divided the word of God. This comes from a lack of believing the bible for what it says. We are in a movement among so called bible believing Christians that say we must always refer to the original Greek and Hebrew to validate the word of God as they believe that God did not do what he said he would do and preserve his word, in its perfect form throughout ALL generations.

The second part is simply pride. We have put all our time and efforts into man-made knowledge and removed our quest of knowledge for the word of God. How dare we say that we need other man-made books to prove to us the bible is real. My bible tells me that faith comes by hearing and hearing by the word of God. I am not in any way against learning from other books. I read a lot of commentaries and there are some that the Holy Spirit has led me to that match up with the bible one hundred percent. My issue is when we place our man-made knowledge higher than the bible then we no longer have faith. this is what those that must refer to the "original" languages are doing.

If as a pastor, you are in a board run church and not a Pastor led church I want to encourage you to seek God for his guidance. Remember God will hold YOU and you alone as the pastor accountable for that church. This we will discuss later in this section. I wat to encourage you pastor, to pastor your church as a God called pastor even if it costs you your job with the board. The reality is you will never change the administration of that board run church at this point it is too late. I would not encourage you to quit that church either. All I am saying is pastor that church Gods way and let him sort it out, what have you got to lose? God will meet your needs.

We now move to question two in this section which is "What are the qualifications of this office?" there is only one reference as to the qualifications that we have in the bible. We see this in *Jeremiah 3:15 And I give will you Pastors <u>according to mine heart</u>, which shall feed you with knowledge and understanding*

According to Gods heart. We must now look at a couple of the attributes of Gods heart as given to us in the bible. As this study continues, we must look to the bible for all our answers. The first attribute of Gods heart that we will look at is love. (I John 4:7-8)

God is love. We hear this all the time in churches, in public places, even with friends and family that we talk to. What is it to actually have a heart of love? We see in John 3:16 that God GAVE his only begotten son. He sacrificed Jesus Christ to save our miserable lost souls from an eternity separated from him in a lake of fire. That my friend is the ultimate act of love. We see another act of love from God through God the Son (Jesus) who despite everything still went to the cross. Even after the horrible beating he suffered prior to the cross. This is love in its truest form. How many of us would actually give our lives or our families lives for people we don't know? Most of us won't even cross the street to tell someone about Jesus.

The bible tells us in *I John 4:7-8 Beloved, let us love one another: for love is of God; and everyone that loveth is born of God, and knoweth God. He that loveth not knoweth not God for God is love*

To know God, is to love. When we speak of love this way, we as Christians must love others UNCONDITIONALLY. A Pastor MUST love others also. A Pastor must love those whom the world deems unlovable, God does, and he says we are to show that love to EVERYONE. Looking at verse 8 we see that if a person does NOT love than he does not know God.

I have seen pastors and wives who have not shown love to others, I have seen those who talk about others when they are not around. It is a sad day that a lot of pastors today are only in a pastorate for the position, for the money, and for the popularity it could bring. These have no love in their hearts for others. If a pastor has no love for people, he does not have the main attribute of Gods heart. God has said very clearly that a pastor that HE calls Must be after his heart.

For a Pastor to have the heart of God he must daily be committed to prayer and study. I'm not talking every minute of the day as there are always sheep that need fed and time must be set aside for that. I'm talking in his alone time. A pastor who does not commit himself to prayer and study is not a pastor going after that Love that God has.

There are pastors in churches across this country who are in these offices of overseers that are not God called but serving in that office anyway God will STILL hold them fully accountable. Therefore, it is crucial for true biblical growth of a flock to have a GOD called pastor and not a man appointed pastor leading a church. You will ALWAYS tell a God called pastor by the fruit in his life. Don't judge the fruit of a pastor by how many people are showing up for church, or how nice the choir sounds, judge a pastor by how the flock turns to God during times of difficulty. If the Pastor has led people to God to solve their problems, then he has the love of God in his life.

Love is the main key to any success in any ministry. Love will be frustrating at times, you as a pastor will invest hours, and sometimes years into a person, just to have them slip back to their old way or leave their walk with God. These times hurt, and they hurt hard, it is during these times that you pray harder for that person. You do not criticize them or get mad at them for long you just love them in spite of themselves. After all God loved you when you were unlovable. Love also will force a pastor to let go of being angry to a person physically and just hold them up in prayer. We read in Proverbs 26:4 not to answer a fool according to his folly. If a person continues to do the same thing over and over again, and keeps going back to the same sin, sometimes you just have to let them go and remove your help from them. They know better and if a pastor has taught them anything about the bible, than James 4:17 comes into effect, *it says him that knoweth to do good and does not do it, IT IS SIN.*

This is where this person, through that pastors loves, must be left to wallow in his or her own folly. Sometimes this even means asking them to not come to church as they will tear apart the flock. The flock belongs to JESUS and the Pastor must tend to that flock

Another attribute we see of Gods heart is righteousness. Righteousness is perfection. A person, Christian, Overseer, etc. will NEVER reach that state of perfection. The bible tells us in Matthew 6:33 to SEEK Gods righteousness. A pastor to be after Gods heart must be doing his best to seek after that righteousness in all he does. My bible tells me that God and sin cannot abide in the same place, and the same time II Corinthians 6:14.

As a pastor seeks Gods righteousness, he must have sin removed from his life. The only way to do that is to "Walk in the Spirit" (Gal. 5:16). Walking in the spirit will require the pastor again to be daily in the word of God and seeking diligently the attributes of Gods heart. A pastor who is walking in spirit will show that fruit in his life. It is important for the Pastor, above all others, to be walking in the spirit, as he is to lead his flock to God, he MUST set that example to his flock for them to follow.

A truly God called pastor will reflect God in his life almost all the time. I say almost because that pastor is human, and we also see in the nine references to pastors that God will also chasten them. God tell us in Jeremiah 23:2 that God will visit the evil of the pastors upon them. A pastor will mess up from time to time, to judge that pastor based on a once in a while slip up, when the overall fruit is evident is not biblical. When God says he will visit their evil upon them this is for those pastors who do NOT repent. If a Pastor is not called by God and does the evil he will not repent as he is not seeking Gods approval of his life but mans.

A searching heart for a pastor is another attribute of the heart of God. We see this in Luke 15 in verse 20-24 the father in the story of the prodigal son was searching for his son, not only was he searching for his son but when he saw his son a "great way off" this father RAN to him and hugged him and kissed him.

Growing up in an independent fundamental Baptist church I can say this is a character trait that was lacking a lot of times. I mean no disrespect for any one person but almost everyone in our church at the time would gossip about or look down on a person who had once come to church, got caught up in the way of the world, and then started to come back.

It is a very sad day that Christians, who are members of churches look down on a lost sheep who is trying to return to the fold. As I read and study my bible with the leading of the Holy Spirit, I see many consistent themes in the bible. One theme I see is once true repentance is offered to God, and God's forgiveness is given to that person, God starts to restore them. They will still face the consequences of their sin whatever that may be, but God restores them. Many Christians do NOT practice this.

I believe in churches, that the attitude of receiving back a lost sheep can be restored if our pastors would be more like this father in this story in Luke 15. If God can accept and restore, then our churches must do the same. My Pastor, Dr. Jim Ellis, who has since gone on to Glory, used to say this phrase all the time "Everything, rises or falls on leadership" this being said our pastors should emulate this attribute of God in their lives, and in their churches.

Don't get me wrong there will be times that a pastor will need to ask a person to leave the church, or not let them come back. These are people who are wallowing in their folly. People who have not shown a change in their lives, people who have not repented and are just causing trouble in their local church. The bible is clear on this point. If a pastor is showing the heart of God in his ministry, the power of God will abide in his ministry, and all those who are playing church, wallowing in folly, etc. will be so uncomfortable, and be so overwhelmed by the conviction of the Holy Spirit that they will run as fast as they can from that church.

We see this searching attribute in the same chapter of Luke in verses 1-11. Jesus asks the disciples which of them, if they lose a sheep does not go after it, and then when they find that sheep, does not throw a party? As there is rejoicing in Heaven over a sinner that repented, one that accepts Jesus as their Savior, there must be rejoicing over the one sheep that returns to the fold. Jesus left the fold to find that one lost sheep. Since Jesus is the rock upon which the church is built it is important that we model his actions

Sometimes when a person leaves a church it is because of sinful choices in their lives and living in that sin the church is the last place they need to be. If pastors would not just oh well, we tried, and continued to communicate with them what a difference this would make. That pastor does not necessarily have to talk to them every day, but maybe just send them a text from time to time saying we are praying for you, maybe send them a personal invitation once a month stuff like that. That pastor would be a searching pastor.

I understand that not all pastors exhibit this attribute, nor is a pastor not called by God if he does not show this particular attribute in his walk with God. These attributes we are studding are to show the heart of God which qualifies a pastor.

As there are many attributes of God demonstrated all through the bible this study is not the place in which we are going to learn about all the bible says about God. That reality is simply that there will never be enough time in this life to list all of Gods attributes. If a person is seeking FIRST the Kingdom of God and His righteousness, then he will be drawing closer to God and God will be drawing closer to him.

When we look at a God called pastor whom God has given after his heart, it is simply a pastor who is seeking God and that is reflected in his actions, conversations, reactions, and all of life's troubles. The bible tells us that the disciples were told that they could see a false prophet by their fruits. I tell you; you can spot a man appointed pastor over a God called pastor by their fruits. The issue is sometimes the God called pastors fruit is only shown a little bit at a time as God is breaking and remolding that pastor to be conformed to the image, he wants for him. While the man appointed pastor may have surface fruit immediately, over the long haul there will be no growth.

If a church or bishop or deacon board votes in a Pastor to fill a vacancy in the pulpit and they are truly seeking God, they will choose the God called Pastor. If they are not seeking God but want a God called pastor and vote in the wrong one in time God will remove that man appointed pastor and replace him with a God called one.

How do we know this? I'm glad you asked, the bible tells us that the church is built on Jesus Christ, and that upon that rock the gates of Hell shall NOT prevail against it. If a man appointed Pastor is pastoring a church without having the call of God on his life GOD will remove that pastor. If God does not remove that pastor, then the gates of Hell are winning. Matthew 16:18

Churches today are closing their door faster than ever in today's world. This is because no one in the church is seeking after God. They want a genie God to come out and give, give, give, but they don't want to give back to God. I tell you this, if there is a GOD called pastor, seeking after God, in the pulpit of a church, that church will not close. The church may get almost to that point where it seems like just one more week is all that is left in store, then God will make his church grow again. If you do it Gods way you will not fail. It is a promise from God and God cannot not lie.

When God called me to Colorado to plant a church, we went almost the first two years with just one person in service. I faced these questions and testing from God. I determined to preach like the place was full and let him sort it out. My job was to plant and water, his job was to bring in the increase. These are extremely trying, soul searching times in a pastor's life, and Satan is right there telling you everything he can to get you to quit or to find another church to pastor. If God had wanted me to pastor a different church, he would have put me there. He called us to this work through thick or thin to do it his way, for the time he wants us to do it.

Last year when we back to Florida for a visit my dad and I had a conversation where he suggested that maybe God had a different church for us to pastor since there was not outward signs of growth for a while. I told him I had thought and prayed about that but I just could not get past the fact that God took us across the country, met every need, was still meeting needs and the church was still going one week at a time but was still going. I told my dad I had promised God if he kept just one person coming, I would keep preaching. I also told my dad there were things in my life that God need to break and remold. I was looking at this ministry as a boot camp and God was getting us ready for the battle. I am happy to say the growth has started as God has allowed his ministry to grow. We are seeing lives changing and souls getting saved.

God will give a Pastor after HIS HEART and you will see that in his life. That is the qualifications we see in the bible for the office of a pastor. That pastor MUST be GOD CALLED not man appointed.

Time now to discuss the responsibilities of a pastor. Along with discussing the responsibilities of a pastor we cannot overlook the accountability that God puts on a pastor as well. This is really one of the only offices of an overseer that God clearly demonstrates the accountability of that office as well as the responsibility. So, we will take this one at a time, so we start with "what is the responsibility of this office?"

The bible gives us three clear responsibilities of a Pastor number one is found in Jeremiah 3:15. God says a pastor is to "feed you with knowledge and understanding. They second responsibility is found in our theme verse Ephesians 4:11 Pastors are to teach. The third responsibility is to run the local church found seven times in Revelation 1:20 we see that the Pastors are called stars of the seven churches and they are to run the local church. These three areas of responsibility we will discuss in detail one at a time

Jeremiah 3:15 And I will give you pastors according to my heart, which shall feed you with knowledge and understanding

The first responsibility in this verse is to feed the sheep. Jesus also told his disciples to feed his sheep. Feeding the sheep is something we can all do as we live our lives Gods way. As people come to us with issues needing advice, we can tell them about Jesus and what the bible says about things.

A pastor has the primary responsibility to feed the flock of which God has placed him to lead. A pastor feeds the flock in many ways. The main way a pastor will feed his flock is through bible preaching. The average person today only goes to church once a week. As a matter of fact, a lot of born-again Christians have stopped going to church as often as they used to go.

This has become a difficult task for a pastor these days to do true feeding of his sheep as they are not coming like they used to. I remember hearing and even going a couple of times to tent revivals and camp meetings at our church and lots of people would show up. We live in an age where a lot of pastors are watering down the bible, they will only preach the "God is Love" side of the bible and the "God is just" side of the bible

The world is no longer hearing Hell being preached, the message of repentance is going by the wayside. This is leading to surface Christians. What I mean by surface Christians are those Christians who go to church, acknowledge Christ in their lives but do not live by faith or trust God to do what he says he will do. We had this discussion at bible study the other night about how people no longer live by faith. say what you want, Christians today live by sight.

Preaching the bible will teach the sheep to live by faith. even a literal sheep has faith in its shepherd. A sheep follows that shepherd, listens to his voice, and follows him. That sheep has no idea where he is going, or what the purpose is to their journey, that sheep has no idea where his food comes from, he just has faith and trust his shepherd.

Pastors today are ridiculed, threatened with their jobs, and brought before their elder boards in most churches and told to not be so hateful by preaching Hell and that people are going there if they do not have Jesus. This is a very sad day we are in that Pastors no longer have the guts to stand up against the popular opinion and shut that down. As I stated there are consequences from God himself for a Pastor who does not feed his sheep, the way they need to.

A pastor feeding of his sheep is more than just preaching the bible the pastor must counsel with people, make hospital visits, perform funerals, and weddings. It is those 2am calls to come to the hospital and be with a family of the church whose son or daughter was just seriously injured or killed in a car accident and getting that family to understand that they need to trust God. When a person is in a very distraught mind set in their lives turning to God is really the last thing they want to do. Most of the time they just want to blame God for the choices they or their family members have made.

Therefore, it is crucial for the pastors to preach WITHOUT APOLOGY the bible and to feed his sheep as much as possible. I mentioned earlier that there is no more faith in our churches today and the only way that can be is because the Word of God is NOT being taught. My bible says that "***Faith cometh by hearing and hearing by the word of God" Romans 10:17.*** I understand this verse is used in the context of a lost sinner coming to salvation but its implication for the saved person is just as valid. As we read and study Gods word our faith increases.

I pity the pastors who have failed on their responsibilities to feed Gods sheep in Jeremiah we see in a few verses that God will scatter their sheep (Jer. 10:21) this verse also tells us that pastors have turned from seeking the Lord. I would have to agree that pastors do not seek God, because if they did there would be faith, love, charity and all other biblical principles being practiced in today's church. All we have in the modern churches are large salaries, multimillion-dollar buildings, with just as much debt, and very large crowds. While five minutes after the service is over people are fighting and cussing out each other in the parking lot as they got cut off leaving the campus. I get annoyed with pastors today who call their churches "campuses" this is not a worldly country club it is supposed to be Gods church.

The verse that hits me the most in Jeremiah is in chapter twenty three and verse two the last part God says "….***behold, I will visit upon you the evil of your doings, saith the LORD"*** let that simmer in your mind for a moment. God will visit upon YOU. This is talking about the pastors because they have not preached the bible, they have not feed the sheep, not have stopped seeking after God. This verse rattled me when I was doing this part of this study. As a pastor I do not want God to visit any sin upon me. I will do my very best to seek God daily in my life. Do I know how to be a Pastor? No, do I know how to feed the sheep? No, but all I do know is that God has called me to Pastor and all I know how to do is to seek him and preach the bible as I go, and he will lead me in pastoring. I have also read II Timothy 2:15 and know I must STUDY to show myself approved unto God.

God says he will VISIT the pastor's evil upon that pastor. Please note, God did not say he will visit the evil upon the elder board, or the voting members of the church he says he will visit the evil upon the PASTORS. This needs to be heeded by pastors if they have accepted that responsibility of pastoring in a local church then they are RESPONSIBLE TO GOD for that church.

Ezekiel 33:1-7 Again the word of the Lord came unto me, saying, Son of man, speak to the children of thy people, and say unto them, When I bring the sword upon a land, if the people of the land take a man of their coasts, and set him for their watchman: If when he seeth the sword come upon the land, he blow the trumpet, and warn the people; Then whosoever heareth the sound of the trumpet, and taketh not warning; if the sword come, and take him away, his blood shall be upon his own head. He heard the sound of the trumpet, and took not warning; his blood shall be upon him. But he that taketh warning shall deliver his soul. But if the watchman see the sword come, and blow not the trumpet, and the people be not warned; if the sword come, and take any person from among them, he is taken away in

his iniquity; but his blood will I require at the watchman's hand. So thou, O son of man, I have set thee a watchman unto the house of Israel; therefore thou shalt hear the word at my mouth and warn them from me.

Let's look in Ezekiel 33 for a moment verses 1-7 give the illustration of a watchman who is to warn the people of the coming enemy and if the watchman fails to warn the people of their pending doom then the blood of the people will be upon the head of the watchman. God goes on to say in verse seven that Ezekiel as the preacher then was told to tell this message to the people. If he had failed at that God would hold Ezekiel responsible for their defeat. Verse eight tells us that God says if Ezekiel failed to warn the people of their iniquity that person will die in their iniquity. Which means they will pay for their own sin as all men will if they reject Jesus but the message is very clear that if Ezekiel did not warn that wicked person that God would blame Ezekiel for that wicked person going to Hell because he was not warned. If we think about that when we as pastors do not warn people of going to Hell without Jesus because it might offend them, WE will be responsible before God for not telling them about Jesus. I don't know about you, but I don't want to have that conversation with God when I get to Heaven.

It is only my opinion that at the Great White Throne judgement that we as saved people will be standing in the courtroom watching as those we have met in our lives, or those in our families, those we have come in contact with in our jobs, church, etc. stand before God and he opens the book of life and says your name is not here depart from me I never knew you. I sometimes think about that moment that person sees their eternity is in the Lake of Fire and just before they are thrown into the Lake of Fire, they look at me and say why did you not tell me?

This, a lot of pastors will have the guilt of dealing with. God says he will VISIT that evil upon that pastor. If you are a pastor and reading this and have been failing to run your church the way God wants you to than start today. Remember the chastisement of man is just a drop in the bucket compared to God visiting your evil or not warning the sheep about the danger of eternity separated from God on you. You, pastor, are accountable to GOD ONLY for how you run your church. Your elder board, or church members will not be standing there with you, you will be there by yourself.

As the remainder of Ezekiel goes as you study this information for yourself you will see God also tells Ezekiel that if he sounds the alarms and warns the people of the enemy, or in today's world the payment for not turning to Jesus and the people do not listen or reject that warning then that person will be responsible to God for not heeding that warning and the pastor/watchman will NOT have that blood on their head.

If you happen to be called to preach and are waiting for God to put you where he wants you and you are reading this book, then heed what is said and start from the very beginning to run your church GOD'S way and not the way of an elder board. Nowhere in the bible is the elder board held accountable to God for the feeding of sheep, but the Pastor always is. FEED YOUR SHEEP as God has said and let God sort out everything else

The second responsibility of the pastor is to teach as we see in Ephesians 4:11 where the bible has pastors and teachers listed as the same person. A pastor will have the ability to tach as part of the gifts God gives to a Pastor he chooses. Teaching is just as crucial as the preaching part of a pastor's ministry as the teaching continues to feed deeper the attributes of God and his love. Teaching equips the saints to go tell others, to live by faith, to trust God without understanding, for everything in life.

Teaching what the bible says will eliminate the tragedy that has happened today in our churches where the devil is no longer fighting against the church, but he is joining them. Teaching the doctrines of the bible will stop the influx of sin from being accepted in our churches, it will stop different versions of the bible that leave verses out and remove the authority of God and Jesus and put that authority on to golden idols. Teaching must be done to protect the kingdom of God and to not let the gates of Hell prevail.

Satan will disguise himself in any way to conquer the church that Jesus died for. Because of the lack of teaching the truth of the bible we have sexual immorality running ramped in our churches, mostly with the members, some with the staff. Pornography and fornication is at an ultimate high among our church leaders in today's world. There is deception in our churches, if you don't believe me just watch any tell-evangelist or any church with a tv show all they want is your money. Because teaching biblical truth has failed in our churches, we have turned from have God be our God to making money be our god. My bible says the "*love of money is the root of all evil*" *I Timothy 6:10.* Other versions of the bible even water down this verse by saying the love of money is A root of all kinds of evil….

Teaching of God's word will keep God as God in our lives, it will keep the exercise of faith in our lives and the bibles says that God is able to do **EXCEEDING ABUNDANTLY *above all we could ask or thing Eph. 3:20.*** Teaching will also keep the flock, the church of God focused on prayer.

Prayer is such a lost art in church today, even in our independent Fundamental Bible believing Baptist churches this art is lost. We go to prayer meetings and spend 45 minutes of our hour long prayer meeting taking prayer requests to have them turn into an actual gossip session just before we go to pray and say some great spiritual words of prayer to impress all who are in the prayer meeting with us. Then we have audacity to question why our prayers are not getting answered.

One of the worst prayer exercises I have ever heard of was when the church I grew up in had what they called a telephone prayer chain. This was where if you had a dire request you would call one person on the phone then they were to call the next one on the list and so on. The idea was that we would pray for that request. Well once the gossip started between the first and second call then that gossip was added to by the third and fourth call, then little Johnny who had initially gone to the hospital for stitches because he cut his arm, was now having open heart surgery by the end of the prayer chain.

God spews this stuff out of his mouth. We as Christians pray vain reputations, and for show without truly seeking God then we wonder why there is no revival, why our kids are going the way of the world. We wonder why our governments are promoting the murder of unborn babies it is because we, yes, we Christians have made such a mockery of prayer. Therefore it is crucial that Pastors get guts and teach the word of God, rebuke sin, stomp on the devil, tell people they will split HELL wide open if they don't turn from their wicked ways. May God have mercy on our souls, and may God have mercy on the pastor's souls who do not lead their churches in true prayer and teach them how to seek God.

Do a test to prove me wrong. This is the challenge for a pastor who wants Gods best for him. Announce on Sunday that your Wednesday night prayer meeting will be a prayer meeting. All churches with a Wednesday night prayer meeting have maybe 10 to 15 minutes of prayer, with one or two people praying for 1 to 2 minutes while the rest is "taking request" and then go on to a short message, then 30 minutes of fellowship after service is over then all go home.

Back to the challenge, take your Wednesday night prayer meeting and as soon as the meeting starts say no prayer requests or announcements, or music tonight just say all who want to pray come to the front and lets start praying then those who don't can stay if they want or can leave if they want. I guarantee you that MOST will leave within ten minutes. Most at the alter will leave in ten minutes. Then pray until the Holy spirt arrives and continue to pray until he says stop. Pastor, do you want the power of God on your church teach them to pray.

If you take this challenge, you will be heartbroken at the response you get, and it will give you more fuel for your personal prayer time and then you can see God start to work. I am not trying to be critical I am just outlining the truth and to show what the bible says are the responsibilities of a pastor.

I actually did this challenge in our church. Now because we do not have a permanent building, we are only able to have services on Sunday for now, but I took a Sunday morning and made it a solid prayer service. I announced it one week before and told the church just how it was going to go that we would show up and just start to pray to God and let him be God and move in our church. This made one of our regular attenders who claimed to be a born-again Christian, spiting fire mad and he refused to come. He said church was for preaching and prayer meeting were for other times than church. I smiled at him and said I understand your point, but my bible says that the Fathers house is to be a house of prayer.

Can you imagine what kind of revival would take place around this world if pastors would make their churches houses of prayer, even if it is just once a month. We would see more souls saved, more lives changed, and Holy Ghost power in our pulpits. Church members will show up in large flocks to support their right to have their guns, they will show up in large flocks to support a political candidate but they will scatter when it comes time to show up for a revival meeting, or a prayer service. Try it, you will be surprised.

Pastors responsibility is to teach the congregation, the bible and ALL it can do for them. We as pastors must teach and practice the bible to our sheep because it teaches THEM to turn to GOD first, not last. On a final note on teaching, remember pastor, it is not about how much you know or how what words you use it is about teaching your flock to turn to God not you for their help. You are just a man and cannot change one thing in their lives, but you can lead them to the one who can. We often forget this, we often go straight to ourselves as being the one who changes their lives, we must keep the cross first and foremost in our lives and churches.

The third responsibility we will discuss in this study is the pastor is to be the head of his church not a board of directors, elders, deacons, or whomever. To do this we will need to go to Revelation chapters 1-3. We will list a couple of verses here and then reference others along the way.

Revelation 1:19-20: Write the things which thou hast seen, and the things which are, and the things which shall be hearafter; The mystery of the seven stars which thou sawest in my right hand, and the seven golden candlesticks. The seven stars are the angles of the seven churches: and the seven candlesticks which thou sawest are the seven churches.

The seven stars are the seven angles. these are the messengers to the churches. The messengers to the church are the pastors that God has put in the local church. The Pastor is the messenger. As we continue to read more of this passage there was a letter written one to each star (pastor) of each church. This is in no way a plural form it is totally singular as you read this passage. You may have looked up in a couple commentaries, but all are consistent that the angles as messengers here are the pastors of these churches. Jesus said to write the letter TO the angel of these churches as these are already at these churches not being sent to these churches.

Since Jesus was the one that told John to write these things down, he did not tell him to write it to the church but to the "angel" of the church. If the pastor was not the head of the church, or the final authority of the church as his God given right was, then why did Jesus not use the word angels plural? He used it singularly to be consistent with the rest of the bible and establish that the pastor is the head of the church not a board of elders.

In this passage of scripture, we also see that there was a warning to these angels to tell their churches to repent or sure destruction would follow, (Rev. 2:5) This is the pastor's responsibility. Pastors you must lead your churches to God, and you cannot do that if you are not in charge of your churches.

The manager of a business is responsible to the owner. How can the owner of the business hold that manager accountable for the store employees being late all the time, taking money, etc. if he does not have the authority to hire and fire who he needs to? How can that manager be held accountable if he does not have total control of that store? For a person to be held accountable he must be allowed to perform his responsibilities without restriction. This is how God has established the church through Jesus Christ. The Pastor is the head of the church and all others in the church are under the authority of that pastor.

I truly believe from scripture that God has given the pastor the liberty to run his local church how he desires to run it as long as he is feeding the sheep, teaching, and leading that church, perfecting the saints for the work of the ministry, and edifying of the body of Christ. (Ephesians 4:12) For example I don't think God cares if a church has ministry directors, or if they call them leaders, if they have one committee or twenty, if they have announcements before the congregational song or after them it just simply does not matter and that is up to the pastor.

All persons, let me emphasize that again, all persons in the local church are under the authority of that pastor and are to willingly submit to that authority as God has set up. This includes Bishops, which we will discuss in the next chapter, Deacons, elders. All positions of overseers in the local church are under that pastor's authority.

We now move on to the fourth question of "who was their ministry to?" We know from the information above that the ministry of a Pastor is to the local church that God has placed him in. a pastor's ministry is not to jump from church to church. I have heard many testimonies of pastors saying I have been at this church for this long, then this one for this long. I do not believe God puts pastors in church for them to jump from church to church.

I do believe that God might put a new pastor in a church for a while for a specific time. This could be for training, for God to teach this pastor a few things about dealing with people, then maybe move him after that, but it would be a rare occasion and would have to be one hundred percent God who initiates the move not that pastor.

One bad habit that we who have surrendered to the complete will of God have is that we want to start serving God with everything we have to the point of getting there before God is ready for us to be there. Several years ago I had surrendered to God to be a Pastor and wanted to get started so bad that I did not wait for God to put me there that I started a church and was in NO WAY ready for that. Well let's say I wish I had waited for God. When that church did not stand the test, I then got mad at God for a while, and well then the true lessons began. Many years later I have learned to wait on God, he is growing his church, and I am very content with what God is doing in my life.

A pastor needs to not have expectations of moving to a mega church, or any other church in a better area or anything of that sort. God put him in the church that he did and wants him to pastor that church. That Pastors entire ministry is to that church. To teach, disciple, manage, and equip the saints for the work of the ministry.

We see in Ephesians 4:11-13 that as God gave some Apostles, prophets, evangelists, and pastors, that he gave them for a specific reason. We have focused on verse 11 now we will go to 12 and 13.

For the perfecting of the saints, for the work of the ministry, for the edifying of the body of Christ: Till we all come in the unity of the faith, and of the knowledge of the Son of God, unto a perfect man, unto the measure of the stature of the fulness of Christ:

God is telling us that the people he called in verse eleven are there to do the work of the ministry, till we meet Jesus face to face, what a glorious day that will be. I did not read in these verses that a God called person listed in verse eleven was to quit, or to move churches. These people are to STAY where God put them until the return of Christ or God himself moves them. Remember in verse eleven the Pastor is the only one listed whose call was to stay with the church and not to travel.

I personally believe that a Pastor has no business even retiring unless physical issues prevent him from pastoring. Again, this is my opinion based on the above verses. I have never heard of retirement in the bible, or of being a certain age and then the work is completed then we are done. No, we do the job God assigned until death.

It is best practice as we get older to delegate the responsibilities of our ministries to those who have the call on their lives and are training under your ministry. The pastor's primary function is to walk with God so he can lead his church to walk with God.

Now we move to the last question "is this office still around in today's evangelical church?" the answer is simply yes. Every church has a pastor, and that pastor should be the head of that church.

6. Bishops

I Timothy 3:1 This is a true saying, if a man desire the office of a bishop he desireth a good work.

As we now go back down the road of Overseers, we come to the next side road of Bishop Ave. everything we discuss from this point forward on the offices of overseers are the internal offices of the local church under the authority of the pastor of the local church. This means all the remaining offices which are bishops, deacons, and elders are appointed by the pastor. We will still discuss the five questions for each office of an overseer, and what their roles are in the local church according to the bible.

This is the most controversial office of an overseer as most people say a Bishop and Pastor are the same office. If you use any other version of the bible beside King James, you can easily come to that conclusion. No other version uses the word bishop but the King James. All other versions take the word bishop and replace it the word overseer, and as the bible is very clear there are many offices of an overseer. So, it leads to a false narrative on qualifications for a Pastor and church leadership.

The word Bishop is used five times in the bible to describe a separate office of an overseer and is never identified in the same category as a Pastor, shepherd, or teacher. We will discuss these verses as this study continues. Again, this is not intended to cause any division in the body of Christ, just simply "rightly dividing the word of truth"

A bishop by definition is simply listed as an "overseer" this is a very vague description as there is no definite office listed for a bishop. When we study the bible, and we don't have clear answers we must then look at what the bible says to come to the best biblical answer that we can. All answers and comments will be coming from the bible itself. Before we get started into this. I ask that you seek the Holy Spirit in prayer for guidance into this office. If you already have your mind set that a Bishop and

Pastor are the same person then I ask you to close this report and don't go any farther, as all this information will most likely do is frustrate you.

I have for many years wondered why there were specific requirements for Bishops and Deacons listed in Timothy and Titus, but the word Pastor was never used in conjunction with these passages. I was reading a commentary on Titus where the author clearly says that a bishop and Pastor are not the same. This comment had sparked what I had been believing for some years, so I needed to put my thoughts to paper and start this study.

I reached out to others who have detailed knowledge of the bible and they say they believe also that a bishop and deacon are the same but not a bishop and pastor. Just saying that because a bishop is defined as an overseer that he is an elder, and therefore is a Pastor is not what the bible says as we have shown that there are different offices of an overseer. As I stated at the beginning of this book, if we consider all overseers as Pastors and hold them to the requirements in Timothy and Titus then we must hold our nursery directors, church secretaries, Sunday school teachers to that same standard as well since they are ALL overseers. To simply say all overseers are the same is wrong and leads to a false biblical doctrine

Let's get started, the first question we ask of all offices of overseers is "how is this office called, by God, or appointed by man?"

I Timothy 3:1 This is a true saying, if a man desire the office of a bishop he desireth a good work.

The first thig we see in this verse is that "If a man desire" this is clearly saying that a man who may be walking with God but that God has not called to be a Pastor wants or feels lead to be a spiritual leader in the local church that he can desire that position. My father says he believes that bishops are deacons are called by God as God impresses upon the pastor to appoint them and since God tells the pastor to appoint them then they are called by God. I understand his thinking on this and do not disagree with it however the actual commissioning of the office is still appointed by man (the Pastor)

This verse tells us that a man either impressed by God to ask the pastor about being in that office, or the pastor impressed by God to appoint that man to the office is still up to the pastor. I want to go one step further and say that nowhere in the requirement of either a bishop or deacon is there any mention of Gods call on the person appointed to that position. A Pastor however had to be called by God. As we stated in the last chapter all church operations and offices of leadership are under the authority of the pastor, and that pastor can appoint whomever he chooses to those offices. The pastor is responsible to God if he puts men in these offices who are seeking God or not.

We will say from this verse the answer to this first question is clearly that a bishop has to be appointed by man if he desires that office and since there is no other mention of the calling of a bishop in the bible we must conclude this to be accurate. If it is not a God called office as those listed in Eph. 4:11 then it CANNOT be the same as the office of a pastor. Also ask the question why did Paul not use the word Bishop, in Eph 4:11?

This verse also says that a man who desires this office desires a good thing. It is good for those who are trying to walk with God, can use what God has taught them to help others. We all have had a person who is struggling come to us at some point looking for hope. To share the hope of Jesus with them is an awesome feeling. We will also have those with false doctrines and beliefs come to us as well and being able to give them answer to what they are saying is good as well. For a person to be in the position of defending the faith they must be on a journey of seeking God. God gives each and every one of us special talents and abilities to accomplish his work, and all our talents and abilities as we have them independently of each other all work for the uniting of Gods people and reaching the lost. The offices of a bishop is a great office to hold and has mostly spiritual responsibilities in the local church.

It is foolish to believe that the pastor can meets the needs of each person in his flock all the time. We see this in Acts where the apostles appointed elders to help minister to the needs of the flock so they could continue with the larger issues. As the pastor appoints people to help him in ministering to each person in his flock he is allowing himself not to get caught up in the daily dramas that arise in life and allows him to focus on prayer, bible study, preaching and teaching the Word of God. It is so easy to get caught up in life's drama that you get your eyes off the cross and place it on the situation. A pastor MUST have help to run the church God has given him, he gets that help by delegation of the minor tasks of the church.

Paul knew this and that was why he told Timothy that as he was to help get the church at Ephesus straightened out, working with the pastor of that church (see chapter on Timothy) that since some of the ministering had to be delegated the people that were appointed to these offices had to meet certain requirements to keep the spiritual emphasis on all matters of life.

This will lead us to the second question of "what are the qualifications of this Office?" talking about being a bishop. There are seventeen requirements for a bishop to meet before he can be appointed to that office.

Before we get to these requirements, we must address the idea of hypocrisy on these requirements. To debunk this, we must say that there is NO respect of persons with God and that sin is sin. Sin can be forgiven once repentance is given to God. I say this because there are many people who believe that if a man has committed the sin of divorce and after his repentance and forgiveness that that disqualifies a person from that position for ever. These same people also say that if a person was drunkard at one time in his life and has now offered repentance and gotten forgiven that he IS qualified for that position. People spend so much time deciding what sins they want to disqualify a person for while at the same time overlooking other sins in other people who are seeking that same office

For example, I have seen a person who has been seeking God with fruit in his life to testify to that, seek the office of deacon and meet all the requirements but in his past when he was in a backslidden state got divorced. Sometime later his life got right with God, but he was told he could never be chosen as a deacon because of this sin he had committed, and there was not much that he would be qualified to do in the church. While at the same time for that same office I have seen a pastor approve a man with no fruit in his life of Gods working, this man being very arrogant, and prideful, having bad business practices in his life, and not of a good report at one time.

It is unscriptural and hypocritical to classify one sin of the seventeen requirements to a higher standard than the other sixteen. This also eliminates God's forgiveness and restoration which I will be doing in one of my next books.[3]

On to the first of the requirements: I Timothy 3:2-7 "a bishop must then be **blameless**…" blameless means without fault. This does not mean that the person must be perfect as no one can be perfect see Romans 3:10, 23. This is simply saying that this person must have the testimony that he is an honest person and that if there were ever to be any accusations against him the first and immediate thought of any person who knows him was that that accusation was false. This is the type of person who when no one is looking still does the right thing. This person will pick up trash in a parking lot if he is walking by it on his way into the store. This person will return the shopping cart to the cart catcher when finished with it. He will be the person you can always expect to be honest and do the right thing in ALL situations.

Requirement number two is to be "the husband of one wife." Man, oh man has this requirement been a battlefield for many Christians throughout the centuries. Many churches have split over this as well as slanders, and heresies being thrown at others for their different comments on this. We will have to go to basic themes in the bible to come to the answer on this one. There is NO

---

[3] See the authors' book: Redemption: A true life Prodigal

satisfactory answer to this requirement. Someone, somewhere, will get upset with this answer but we must address this in this book. I will do my best not to drag it out too long.

So, let's get started, **"The husband of one wife"** there are conflicting opinions on this point. There are those who say a man cannot be divorced and re-married as that constitutes adultery. And there are those who hold the opinion that this is referring to Polygamy. I hold to the latter opinion.

To determine the answer, we must look at what the bible says. This will be a slippery slope no matter how we put it and I will not go into extreme detail now, but I will in my first book[4]

The bible tells many stories in the bible of men having several wives. We see Solomon for example having seven hundred not to mention the concubines. Then we see Jacob had Rachel and Leah. This was a common practice in this time and all through scripture. At the time of this writing of Timothy the bible was not complete, and they were going off old testament scripture. This leads to the question "was Polygamy a sin?" the answer to that would have to be NO.

---

[4] See the Authors book: The Biblical Family: From Beginning to Blended

We will refer to **Exodus 21:10 If he take another wife; her food, her raiment, and her duty of marriage, shall he not diminish.** Polygamy, though not the intent was allowed by God. Since it was allowed it was not a sin. It was part of the culture of that time.

The other view of the requirement was divorce and remarriage was adultery and therefore considered a continual act of adultery. This in my understand of the word of God is a misrepresentation of what God is saying. If this were true, the only way for a remarried person to stop sinning is to sin again by divorcing the wife they remarried.

So let's look at some more verses. **Matthew 5: 31-32. 31 it hath been said, Whosoever shall put away his wife, let him give her a writing of divorcement: but I say unto you, that whosoever shall put away his wife, saving for the cause of fornication, causeth her to commit adultery: and Whosoever shall marry her that is divorced committeth adultery.**

We must look at a couple of things here. Number one is that we see there is a difference in "Putting away his wife" and "giving her a writing of divorcement". Putting away a wife is a separation from that wife. This is important to note that if you use other versions of the bible besides the King James many of them have changed the "putting away of his wife" and replaced it with Divorced. This will lead to a contradiction when you get to the scriptures in I Corinthians 7:27-28 This was common practice of that time for a man to separate from his wife and marry another if she was divorced. I have always wondered why it was considered adultery if you married a divorced person. A separated woman is NOT free to marry. the husband causes the separated wife to commit adultery by not giving her a divorce, when another man comes to marry her, they are then living in adultery. The second thing we must look at here is the "Whosoever" this is referring to the husband and if he remarries a woman that is divorced, he is committing adultery, not because she is divorced, but because he is not. He has not issued her a bill of divorcement. Before you rake me through the coals for heresy, we must look at a couple of more verses of scripture. *I Corinthians 7:27-28 Art thou bound unto a wife? Seek not to be loosed. Art thou loosed from a wife? Seek not a wife. But if thou marry, thou hast not sinned; and if a virgin marry, she hath not sinned. Nevertheless*

*such shall have trouble in the flesh: but I
spare you.*

We see in this passage of scripture that Paul is
saying to focus on the things of God much
better, it would be better not to marry because
when you get married you have to focus some
on worldly things to provide for the wife and
family. These verses in particular are talking
about a married man. If he is married, he is not
to seek a divorce. I do believe that all divorce is
a result of sin, not necessarily adultery, but of
some kind of sin. It is also saying that if a man is
loosed FROM a wife that it is NOT a sin to get
married.

There are those who think this verse is referring
to a man who was never married as being
loosed from a wife, if that were the case it would
not say "Loosed FROM a wife" (capitals added
for emphasis). So to conclude we must rightly
divide the Word of truth, and to that we must say
this requirement for a bishop is referring to one
wife at a time Polygamy was not a sin but
common practice and since getting remarried
after being divorced is NOT a sin. And Paul who
wrote both Corinthians, and Timothy, he would
not write conflicting statements. The one last
point as in the last part of the above verse, the

131

person who has been re-married will have more trouble in his life than a person only married once. This is a result of the divorce. other children will be introduced, so you will now have broken families to deal with. This will cause additional stresses on the second marriage. We also know that a woman cannot be a bishop as she cannot be the HUSBAND of one wife.

The third requirement of a bishop is for that bishop to be **vigilant.** He is to be watchful over the flock. The bishop as an under shepherd is to help watch for false doctrines being introduced into the church, watch for the areas of a person's life where Satan wight be able to divert that sheep from their walk with God. As the Pastor feeds the church as a collective whole the bishops help with the one on one ministering of the flock. The bishop must be vigilant.

The fourth on the list is **Sober.** A Bishop must be of a serious mind set when it comes to serious matters in the church and the ministration of the people there. I do believe it is ok to have a sense of humor when the time is appropriate as the bible tells us much laughter is good for the soul.

The fifth is **of good behaviour,** this is simply actions of this person. If this person has a sober mind his actions will reflect that. He will behave respectfully, lovingly, and caring with those to whom he is to oversee in the church. Sixth is **given to hospitality**, this will reflect his good behaviour as he will demonstrate that love to others. This is simply loving all people. In the ministry people will use you, treat you badly, talk bad about you, you just love them, pray for them, and keep on keeping on.

Number seven is **apt to teach,** apt meaning to be ready, the bishop needs to be ready to teach when needed to. I believe that this role would be in a Sunday school setting, or a small group setting. The bishop could also fill the gap when the pastor is out due to vacation, sickness, or traveling.

Number eight is **not given to wine**, not a drunkard. There is a lot of controversy in the church today over, is drinking a sin or not. The Bible says we are not to be "drunk with wine" (Eph 5:18) it does not say we cannot drink, nor does the bible say a person cannot smoke. But let's be clear these are NOT good habits to have in ministry, these will be a stumbling block for new believers and make things very difficult for the person that does them. The bible says to come OUT from among them and be separate, says the Lord. I believe God will not bless the person who engages in these activities to his fullest

Number nine is **no striker,** this person is not to always want to fight others, he is not quick to hit someone who upsets him. He does not show a violent side. You can tell sometimes if a person has tendencies to be violent just by listening to them talk. He should not always be argumentative with people

Ten, **not greedy of filthy lucre,** lucre is simply defined as monetary gain. This person must not be greedy, always looking how to get more money. It is not a sin for a church leader to have money, but to get greedy about it is. We see this a lot with televangelists and large churches. If a person is focused on money, at some point, they will not be honest and try to get more. I believe if a person is going to be in ministry they need to demonstrate living by faith, if God blesses them greatly with money, then great. A person in ministry or church with a lot of money who is seeking God will be a giver, plain and simple.

Eleven, **patient,** this would mean this person is gentle. He would exercise wisdom in situations.

Instead of getting worked up over a situation he would basically be calm on the whole thing

Twelve, **not a brawler** this is talking about that person that is always loud when things go wrong. Whether this person is upset and trying to fight with someone, or they are making loud negative comments. these are the people that when they are upset, they want everyone to know about it. Usually they end up looking foolish.

Thirteen, **covetous** this is saying that a person who is seeking this office needs to not be motivated by money. They should be content with what they have. If a bishop is seeking God and has faith, he will know that God will meet his needs. I have never heard of a bishop or even deacon in a church getting paid to do that job. I'm sure somewhere that some do but their overall attitude should not be about wanting money, or possessions, or having nicer things, just be content with what God has given them.

Fourteen, **ruleth his own house** this is a requirement that can cause a little dissension in the bible believing world. It does sadden my heart that the body of Christ has SO MANY things they allow to cause divisions in the church. There are no set regulations on what this means to rule your own house, so we go to the bible and see the principles that God placed in there for the family. Is what I mean is that if little Johnny does not have a coat and tie on in church than that bishop is not qualified to be a bishop. There are some who believe that this is what that means.

The bible talks about the basic family structure of the husband leading the home. He provides for them, he loves them, he leads them in all spiritual matters, he is the head (not dictator) of the house as Jesus is the head of the church. The wife the bible says is to be in subjection to her husband. She is to freely of her own will submit to the leadership of her husband. Today's family, the fathers are either gone or lazy and the women have had to lead the homes. The wife is to care for the house, and the children. She is to run the household, and to teach the children.

Fifteen, **having children in subjection with all gravity** the bishop is to teach his children to follow God also. The children are to be taught to obey, to learn to deal with life's issues, to respect and love others. To follow the principles of the bible so when they are older, they will not depart from them. Proverbs 22:6 says it is for the children being in Subjection. ***Proverbs 22:6 Train up a child in the way he should go: and when he is old, he will not depart from it.*** This is talking about children, not adults. There is not a set age limit in the bible as to when a child stops being a child and starts becoming an adult. This would need to be based on maturity. After all, there were what we consider kids today 11, 12, 13 years sometimes getting married and having kids of their own in old times, so it just depends on the child's maturity level.

Sixteen, **not a novice** the person who desires the office of a bishop should not be a new Christian, or a Christian that has recently come back from the "pig pen" as the prodigal son did. The person should be one who has demonstrated their walk with God and there has been evidence of fruit in their lives as to that. They need to be someone who has basic knowledge of bible principles. A person who is mature more in the faith that the average Christian.

Seventeen, **a good report of them which are without** this person must have the evidence with the lost people of the world that he is Christian. We all have people in our lives, jobs, and families. Do they know we are Christians, do we treat them with respect and love especially when they criticize us or our faith? if we were brought to court to be convicted of being a Christian, would there be enough evidence with the lost of the world to convict you?

These are the requirements for a bishop. I want to point out a couple of things with these requirements. One is that did you happen to notice a constant theme? All these requirements are dependent on each other. For example, if a man is a drunkard, he then will not be given to hospitality, or have good behavior. He will not have a good report with those that are lost. As there is a constant theme it has to start with walking in the spirit and you shall not fulfill the lust of the flesh (Gal. 5:16)

If a person who is seeking a bishop office is walking with the Lord all the requirements will fall into place, and you will see the evidence of that in their lives, at church, work, and home.

The second point I want to make is in these requirements for a bishop there is no mention of a call of God on this person. With a pastor the bible very clear that God calls pastors. Since there is no mention of a call of God on this person, but as long as he is qualified in these requirements, he can be a bishop. This is more evidence that the office of a bishop, and the office of a pastor are different. There are many men in our churches today who are walking with God, whom God has not called to preach who are great bishops, and deacons. There are some who can teach, preach, and minister but who are not called to be pastors. There IS a difference between a preacher and a pastor.

At the end of the day the pastor has been granted the privilege of appointing whomever he wants to whatever office of an overseer in the local church, as God has placed him in charge of that church. Just as in the beginning of time God gave man dominion over the earth to subdue it, the pastor has dominion over his church. He is accountable to God and if he appoints a person that is not walking with God then he will have to answer to God for that.

One last point before we move to the responsibility of a bishop, if a person that is seeking the office of a bishop has not met the requirements in his past but at the time he is seeking that office has shown evidence of the Holy Spirit in his life he can, in my opinion, be considered for that office. On the flip side if a person currently in the office of a bishop fails to maintain these requirements of a bishop the pastor should work with him to try to restore him, as the bible says. (Gal. 6:1) if at that point this person cannot be restored the pastor should have him step down from that position for such a time as the issues can be resolved. Again this is between this person and the pastor. If the pastor is wrong in his decisions, he will answer to God for that, remember God will visit his sin upon him, as he did with Jonah and many others in the bible.

Now we can get to the third question we ask of every office of the overseer, this office being a bishop. "What is the responsibility of this office?" this question is where the biggest division comes to light in the Christian church today. The whole basis to this book and the foundation to rightly divide the word of truth will be determined on which version of the bible one chooses to use.

This is NOT a study on other versions of the bible, nor is it any attempt to slam anyone who is not King James. This is simply stating facts, which I strongly encourage you to see for yourself. ALL other versions of the bible change the word bishop to overseer in I Timothy and

Titus. The King James is the only version which uses the word bishop.

Why is this crucial? because one-word change can affect the doctrine of a bible. I have heard this said many a times in church services but have never actually seen the doctrinal impact one-word change can have, until I started this book.

The difference is the word bishop identifies a single office of an overseer, whereas the word overseer is a general term used for many different offices. Let's break this down a little in the main-stream denominations (non-King James) the word overseer can be a Deacon, a Pastor, an elder, or anyone in any position of an overseer. As we talked about at the beginning of this book, any person who oversees any person, or persons property other than their own is an overseer. In essence, the nursery director could also be the pastor of the church.

If you are not a King James person then this section will most likely upset you as you will not see the individual identity of this office, all you will see is the collective identity of this office. I cannot change your view on this nor can I make you be King James only; all I can do is challenge you to seek the Lord first then do this study for yourself.

This one word makes the biggest change I have come across yet. As I stated in the beginning, I am King James only without apology. So, we will move forward with the responsibilities of the office of a bishop from the biblical foundation using the King James version as we have this entire study.

An office of a bishop by definition is an overseership office. It is to oversee the spiritual matters and doctrines of the church. In the modern-day church this position has been merged with the deacon office of an overseer. The bishops were the spiritual leaders in the church. Their function was to help the pastor teach the flock. As the pastor teaches the collective church, the bishops were to teach the individual sheep of that flock. These would be the ones that pastor just did not have the time to do. The bible does tell us what the job of this office was for that answer we will need to go to the book of Titus 1:5-11

Titus 1:5-11 For this cause left I thee in Crete, that thou shouldest set in order the things that are wanting, and ordain elders in every city, as I had appointed thee: If any be blameless, the husband of one wife, having faithful children not accused of riot or unruly. For a bishop must be blameless, as the steward of God; not selfwilled, not soon angry, not given to wine, no striker, not given to filthy lucre; But a lover of hospitality, a lover of good men, sober, just, holy, temperate; Holding fast the faithful word as he hath been taught, that he may be able by sound doctrine both to exhort and to convince the gainsayers. For there are many unruly and vain talkers and deceivers, specially they of the circumcision: Whose mouths must be stopped, who subvert whole houses, teaching things which they ought not, for filthy lucre's sake.

For this cause left I thee in Crete, that thou shouldest set in order the things that are wanting, and ordain elders in every city, as I had appointed thee: If any be blameless, the husband of one wife, having faithful children not accused of riot or unruly. As with Timothy, Paul gave similar instructions to Titus who was at the church at Crete to help get them back in order and to help ordain elders in the church to assist the Pastor.

For a bishop must be blameless, as the steward of God; not selfwilled, not soon angry, not given to wine, no striker, not given to filthy lucre; But a lover of hospitality, a lover of good men, sober, just, holy, temperate; Holding fast the faithful word as he hath been taught, that he may be able by sound doctrine both to exhort and to convince the gainsayers. Unlike in Timothy Paul goes into more detail as what the actual responsibility of the Bishop is. In the bible one has sometimes to read different passages to get the full understanding of what is being taught. Take the Gospels for example you must read and study all four to get all the details of the life of Jesus.

In this passage it says a bishop is to exhort and convince the gainsayers. It is not to feed the sheep, as a Pastor does, it is not perfect the saints for the work of the ministry, it is to rebuke the gainsayers. Gainsayer simply defined is: to declare to be untrue. There were those in the church who were promoting a false gospel, convincing the members of the church that the gospel was wrong. The bishops were to be the ones to rebuke these gainsayers. By having a Bishop in place for this, as he challenged the gainsayers, it allowed the Pastor to feed the sheep, to instruct them in the word of God, to teach them sound doctrinal truth. This is the responsibility of a Bishop in the bible. It has today been eliminated in the church and the Pastor must add this to his responsibility of leading the church.

For there are many unruly and vain talkers and deceivers, specially they of the circumcision: Whose mouths must be stopped, who subvert whole houses, teaching things which they ought not, for filthy lucre's sake. There were many of them in the church that were causing untruths to be spread. Did you also notice that Paul instructed Titus and Timothy to appoint Bishops for this task and for them to do it themselves? If they were the acting Pastors in that church, and a Pastor and Bishop are the exact same, then why would Paul have them appoint people to do this when it would have been their job and just not tell them themselves to do it. It is because a Bishop and a Pastor are two separate positions in the church, and the bishop is under the Pastor for the sake of rebuking false teachers. all churches should have some trained in rebuking false teachers so they can assist the Pastor in this role so he can feed the sheep.

In my bible dictionary it says that a bishop is a spiritual overseer or superintendent. The role of the bishop was also to assist the pastor in the spiritual application of the bible to the individual lives of the people in the church. We all know it is almost impossible for the pastor himself to physically work with each person individually each day to help them apply the spiritual concepts he has preached about. So the pastor appoints bishops to assist in that area.

Bishops are to assist the pastor they are NOT pastors. I will make this point with *I Peter 2:25 For ye were as sheep going astray; but are now returned unto the Shepherd and Bishop of your soul.*

This is talking about Jesus who gave his life for us. That we were lost sheep and have now been returned to the Shepherd (pastor) and Bishop (overseer) of your soul. If shepherd and bishop are the same office, then shouldn't this verse read returned to the shepherd and shepherd of your soul? Shouldn't it say returned to the overseer and overseer of your soul? It says Shepherd AND Bishop of your soul. May I refer you back to the theme verse on this study Ephesians 4:11 "Pastor and teacher" it is the same person filling two different offices. Just as

Jesus is referred to as the great shepherd, he is also a bishop over us. Jesus is our Pastor that he feeds us and gets us ready for the ministry and as our Bishop he rebukes the false teachers that come in our lives.

The best illustration I can come up with for this is Jesus himself. Jesus as the Shepherd in I Peter 2:25 is the pastor to His church the collective church the body of Christ. He preaches to this body, he teaches, this body, and he prays for this body of believers. If we study Jesus ministry as God the Son, we see it was mostly to the masses, most of the sermons he preached were to the crowds. Jesus very little in his role of the shepherd dealt individually with people, and when he did it was brief. Let's look at Zacchaeus, this was a man that Jesus went to his house. Jesus spent some individual time with him in his house. Zacchaeus got saved and his family. However Jesus did not spend that individual time with him after his salvation to help him apply the bible to his life. Jesus as the Shepherd (Pastor) spent his time in prayer and ministering the word to his sheep (the collective church). It is after salvation that God the Holy Spirt then comes into each person and ministers to them individually, thus filling the role of a bishop in the collective church.

The Holy spirit opens our hearts to receive the word that is preached, the Holy spirit tells us how to apply it to our lives, and the holy Spirit calls us out when we sin and are doing things wrong. the Holy Spirit is the overseer of spiritual matters in our lives, just as the bishops are in the local church.

God the son, was the shepherd/pastor while God the Holy Spirit was the bishop of the collective church. In the local church the pastor would appoint several bishops who met the qualifications above and assign them to certain tasks to assist him. They may have had the responsibilities of teaching Sunday school, or teaching small groups, maybe ministering in the jails, no one knows the exact roles that were assigned to them we just know that these two roles are not the same office of an overseer. (I Peter 2:25)

The fourth question we must ask about this office of a bishop is "Who was their ministry to?" that is a simple answer. Their ministry was to the local churches that they were ordained to serve in. if we go to Timothy and Titus we see that they were to ordain bishops and deacons (elders) in the churches they were in and Titus was told to ordain elders in EVERY city in which he went.

The bishop is to be in the local church. The pastor could use the bishop maybe to help another church that is getting started, to go to the mission field and assist a missionary for such a time. There were never just one bishop or spiritual leader in the church, the phrase the bible uses when talking about elders is always plural. We will discuss the office of the elder in a later chapter. A bishop could also fill the pulpit in the absence of the pastor for illness, or vacation. The bishop was under the authority of the pastor. The only time that the bishops of a local church should have any authority in the church operation is if the pulpit is empty. If the pastor has died or retired. Then and only then should the bishops who are already walking with God in their lives, take on the shepherd role, only with the function of filling that pulpit until a new Pastor is put in place. As one who has to stand against false teachers it was crucial that a Bishop was walking with God, that he knew the Word of God and that he help individually to teach the people in the church the word of God.

A pulpit is vacant, the bishops then form a small group and look for a God called pastor and call that pastor to candidate for the church. If that pastor is God called the bishops will see the power of God on his life and in his preaching. If they want this candidate to be the pastor, I believe that God will tell the bishops who he wants in that pulpit. And then they hire this person to be their pastor, then the authority that the bishops had is then gone as there is now a pastor in place. This should be how it works.

This whole idea of letting the sheep pick its shepherd in not a biblical concept. I am very saddened to say that as of right now my church is set up this way also. Set up to where the people, the members, get to vote on who THEY want for their pastor. They can also vote out a Pastor if they so desire. Since this is not a biblical concept but a man-made concept, I will be diligently working to remove these parts from the by-laws of our church's constitution. I will be through prayer and fasting teaching the members what the bible says, and they will vote on removing these clauses of the bylaws.

This is a task that if anyone else tries to attempt you will have to understand that there will be those who oppose surrendering their control of the church and giving it back to God. They will also use bible verses to support their resistance.

You may not win that battle. For me I am going to operate as if these clauses to vote in and out a pastor are not in there and run our church under the leadership of the Holy Spirit Gods church that he gave to his son Jesus. I am also going to add to the bylaws a clause that only in the event of a vacant pulpit is the deacon board to have the temporary authority to hire a new pastor and there will be biblical principles they will have to follow.

In certain events in a local church it is necessary to have other spiritual leaders to help in seeking God for a decision, or direction the church needs to go. this is operating on faith. if a pastor is chasing God, the leadership will chase God. If the leadership is chasing God, the congregation will also chase God and then revival can happen. Just operate your church Gods way and let him do the rest.

The last question of this office is "is this office still around in today's evangelical church?" the answer is yes but only is some denominations. There are some churches who are elevating their senior pastors to a non-biblical bishop position as the Catholic church does. They say the bishop is over the Pastors, and in some cases over several churches. I read an article just yesterday how in a Baptist denomination that the pastors being elevated to Bishops by the church congregation, wearing special expensive rings and robes to identify as a bishop, and they said it made them feel closer to God. To that my friend I say HOGWASH. If you want to feel closer to God just draw nigh to him, he will draw nigh to you.

Most evangelical churches have eliminated the actual title of Bishop and combined it with a Pastor and Deacon role of the church. If you walk into ANY church in America and say a Deacon, the first and immediate thought is a spiritual leader of a church. We will be discussing Deacons in the next chapter.

In the modern-day church the deacon is the bishop, and they are assigned tasks by the pastor to help to minister to the flock of the local assembly. I used to think that the deacon was the second highest spiritual leadership in the church under the pastor. After this study I am learning the truth of the bible. Here is the last thing about the office of the bishop. It is up to the Pastor of the church to run that church however he feels the Lord is leading him. It is up to him if he chooses to use the title Bishop, or deacons or director for those he appoints to assist him in the ministering of the church. If as a pastor you want Gods best on you and your church then set it up and run it Gods way at the end YOU, not a Board, not your congregation, are accountable to God for your church.

7. Deacons

As we now go back down the road of Overseers, we come to the next side road called Deacon drive. The term Deacon simply defined is: a helper, an assistant. This office is seen first established in Acts 6:1-7 this story was that the Grecians were complaining to the apostles that their widows were being neglected in their daily needs. As we have determined in previous chapters that the apostles could not possibly stay to meet the daily needs of the individuals on a daily basis. Their job was to get the gospel and doctrines to the masses and to plant local churches

The apostles called the disciples together to tell them they had to find some men in the crowd of good report and appoint them to this daily task. So they appointed seven men for this task. These seven men, Deacons, were helpers, they assisted the apostles. Churches today still appoint helpers, Deacons, to help in the daily administration of the churches. This is a vital role.

The word Deacon appears only five times in the bible four of which are used in I Timothy for the description of the requirements of being a deacon. The other mention of the word Deacon is in Philippians 1:1. Paul is writing to the church at Philippi he is addressing this letter to all the saints at this church, and also to the bishops and deacons which are in this church as well. The book of Philippians seems to be more of a book of encouragement and how to maintain victory during times of discouragement, suffering, and lowliness.

All Christians need to be encouraged during difficult times. I know from personal experiences that serving in ministry can at times be discouraging, and monotonous. This book keeps those in the offices of service, along with the believers, encouraged to keep on keeping on.

The office of a deacon is a vital function of any local church. These are the get-er-done people of the ministry. Well at least they should be. As with any office of a church or any Christians walk with God, prayer must be a functional part of that position. If a person is not walking with God how can they lead the saints of God to God, how can they lead the lost to God? To emphasis again to walk with God does NOT mean one is perfect or has a perfect past. It simply means there is fruit in his life that he is living the way the bible describes to the best of his ability. A deacon, like ANY OTHER office of an overseer could have at one time in his life, not met any of the qualifications listed in the bible, and still be able to serve in that position today. This is at one time they were sinning or got away from God. Then after their pig-pen experience came back to the Father through true repentance and have been restored. Look through your bible for yourself, it is ALL about repentance and restoration that my friend is the TRUE doctrine of grace. God ABSOUTLY loves using broken people to accomplish his will. I have often wondered why he does use broken people like me and have concluded that those of us who have been broken and have returned have experienced the grace of God on a more intimate level. This is where I use the phrase "a faith that has not been tested, cannot be trusted."

I have mentioned in the previous chapter that at the time a person is considered for any office of an overseer is when the qualifications apply to them. How can we as people hold a person's past against them, if God has already forgiven and forgotten their sins? Psalms 103:12. For those of you pastors looking to appoint people to offices of bishops and deacons just remember to only look at the fruit of their lives, does the FRUIT reflect the requirements? If God has forgiven their past how dare we not!

Now we get to the first question of this office "How is this office called, by God, or appointed by man?" we see in I Timothy 3:8 the word "Likewise" means in like manner, the same way. So, we see that the office of a deacon is an appointed office by the pastor of that church. Since this office is appointed by the pastor the deacon is accountable to the pastor. Therefore, the requirements are listed for a bishop and deacon is so they can be held to that standard.

When a person is held to a certain standard, they know what their expectations are, and usually strive with all their might to achieve those standards. This is a great thing when we see people striving to accomplish biblical goals, and standards. The bible makes reference to whatever you do, do it with all your might. Ecc. 9:10.

When a pastor talks to a person he is interested in making a bishop or deacon he usually lays out this standard set in Timothy, if that person is willing to accept this office they will stay walking with God to maintain these standards for Gods glory. This is only determined by the FRUIT they are producing in their lives. I have seen Many times where NON-FRUIT producing people were appointed to these offices, who all they do is gossip, and live like the world outside of church. With no fruit producing, they put on the image of meeting those requirements and were appointed to those offices, hence the church will not grow, and the pastor will answer to God for those choices.

It really is a simple concept. Especially laid out in Timothy for these requirements, the concept is this: if the pastor is chasing God, the leadership he appoints will be chasing God, if the leadership is chasing God the church will be chasing God, if the church is chasing God the lost will want to chase God. It ALL rises and falls on leadership.

The second question is: "what are the qualifications of this office? We need to turn back to I Timothy 3:8 to see the requirements. On a side note the book of Titus does not list any requirements for a Deacon only a bishop, we will discuss that farther in the chapter on Titus. These requirements are a little different and not as many as listed for a bishop. A bishop had 17 qualifications, but a deacon only has nine.

Number one is the deacon must be grave. Grave means to be worthy of respect. A person who has shown respect to others, and has a great attitude, one who can exercise wisdom in some situations. This person is worthy of respect.

Number two is NOT doubletongued. This man shows that he says one thing and does it. He does not say he is your friend then goes to John Smith on the other side of the church and say you are an evil person. He does not say he cares for the lost then ignores the homeless family in front of the store. He says what he says and does what he says.

Number three not given to much wine. Again, like with a bishop, this is an area that in my opinion, lukewarm Christians struggle with. They believe it is ok to drink just as long as you don't get drunk. The mature Christian will have the personal conviction that abstinence from any strong drink is the best testimony one can set for God. We must refer to the bible for the final clarity on the subject of drinking. *I Corinthians 6:12 All things are lawful unto me, but all things are not expedient: all things are lawful for me, but I will not be brought under the power of any.*

Paul was saying it might not be a sin to drink strong drink, or smoke cigarettes, or do other things that Christians say you cannot do, but there is no actual reference in the bible to those things, it is better to abstain from them then to be brought under the power of them. I will say, Satan is waiting for Christians to engage in these questionable acts so he can get you under the power of them. I have not ever met a person yet who once they have had alcohol or smoke, they don't get caught under the power of it in some form. Best practice is to abstain. Most churches who have deacons make it a requirement that no drinking is allowed. The average church going Christian expects the leadership to NOT drink strong drink

Number four not greedy of filthy lucre. As with anything in life there is always a temptation for money, after all, it is said that money makes the world go around. The person qualifying for this office must not have the desire to gain money at any cost. This is a horrible testimony to any church. Unfortunately, we see this in a lot of churches and denominations who the only thing you ever hear preached is Money, or Give, give, give. This kind of actions destroys the kingdom of God and drives the lost so far away from church and God that it is extremely difficult for those truly spreading the gospel to get their message out.

Number five the deacon must have faith. this was not in the qualifications for a bishop, however if a person is walking with God their faith will increase. I want to look at Acts 6:3-5. ***Acts 6:3-5 Wherefore, brethren, look ye out among you seven men of honest report, full of the Holy Ghost and wisdom, whom we may appoint over this business. But we will give ourselves continually to prayer, and to the ministry of the word. And the saying pleased the whole multitude: and they chose Stephen, a man full of faith and of the Holy Ghost, and Philip, and Prochorus, and Nicanor, and Timon, and Parmenas, and Nicolas a proselyte of Antioch:***

When the apostles were choosing the initial seven people to help meets the needs of the crowd, the seven deacons, elders, they had to be men filled with the Holy Ghost, and wisdom. This comes from having faith, we see in verse five that one of the men they chose was Stephen who was FULL of faith. faith is a qualification for the office of a deacon as well as Pastors should make it a qualification for any office they assign to the church.

In Ephesians 4:11 where he gave some Apostles, prophets, evangelists, and pastors, all of them had to live by faith and walk by faith. it is foolish for a pastor to put a person into an office who has not demonstrated faith in their lives. *1 Timothy 3:10 And let these also first be proved; then let them use the office of a deacon, being found blameless*. In this verse of I Timothy Paul is saying to prove that man to see if he has faith. Then once his faith has been proved he can then fill the office of a deacon. This is not saying to force this person into a car take them to the middle of the Sahara Dessert and drop them off with just their clothes and shoes and tell them to find their way back to the church. Although I see a movie in the making with that story line. This is saying to the pastor to watch this man for a time, does he live his life by faith, does he seem to trust God in all his life, does he give tithe to the Lord by faith trusting

God to meet his needs? Then once that has been determined then he can occupy that office.

You can watch a person as much as you want, and it is possible to appoint a person to an office like this who puts on a show of faith but does not truly have faith. these will slip through the crack from time to time, but when it is revealed the pastor needs to replace or remove that person as they will cause more damage to that church than you can imagine. If the pastor is chasing God, God will lead him to appoint the right people to the correct offices.

This will make the deacon to be found blameless in all he does. A man that exercises and walks by faith in God in his life will always do the right thing. And if there is a time where he does not do the right thing, he will make it right immediately upon learning he did the wrong thing. This is how it works with God. The closer you get to God the more the things of God become the desire of your heart.

The number six qualification for a deacon is about their wives. There was no mention of the role a wife plays in the office of a bishop but there are direct instructions for a deacon's wife. I wondered why this was and after talking with the

Lord he showed me it is because the office of a Bishop deals with doctrine and spiritual leadership, the deacon deals with the practical leadership. The hands-on leadership. The office of the deacon was to work with the people one on one. When working one on one you get to know the people. As you get to know people you get to know all their business. And knowing all their business is not for you to go tell everyone you see about it. This is called GOSSIP. Gossip runs rampant through a lot of churches today. And men tell their wives things in confidence and both sometimes tell others which turns into gossip.

I believe that because of the knowing of the business of others is why there are instructions for the wives here as well. A wife is to assist her husband if he is a deacon, she should be assisting him in ministering to the people of the church. If her personal walk is with God, she will have the heart of love and help not of deceit and gossip.

A deacon's wife must be grave, as we saw with the deacon, is to be worthy of respect. She is to not be slanderous, there it is, not to gossip, not to talk bad about others. She is to be sober. She is to have a clear mind, sober thoughts and a heart focused on God. In case you have missed it, this is all about a person's walk with God. She is to be faithful in all things. This includes her walk with God, her love for her husband, and her love for others.

Number seven on the qualification list is for the deacon to be the husband of one wife. We discussed the "one wife" in the last chapter so we will not go back there in this one. I will however address one thing I did not do in the last chapter and that is why are the offices of an overseer an office designed for a man. Why can't women hold these offices biblically? I use the term biblically because you will see in some churches that women are pastors, women are elders, women are deacons, etc. This is because people have chosen not to believe the bible and only apply the parts they like to their lives and ignore the rest. Again, as stated in the chapter on Pastors whomever is serving in the office of a pastor whether man or a woman-unbiblically, is accountable to God himself and God will visit their sin upon them, enough said on that. The bible tells us that a woman is NOT to usurp authority over a man I Timothy 2:9-13. This was Gods design; he created the man FIRST then the woman. The man is held accountable for the family not the woman. The woman was created to be HELP MEET (Genesis 2:18)

When a woman oversees a church, she is not submitting to the authority that GOD himself established, and therefore is rebelling against God. God has never said in the bible that a woman could not do what a man can do. He designed it his way and that was for the man to be the leader, the protector, the provider. Just as with the Abrahamic covenant where God said Jacob have I loved, Esau have I hated. He was not saying that those of the tribe of Esau were condemned to Hell and there was no possibility for them to turn to him and repent. He was saying that between the two of them he chose Jacobs blood line for the Son of God to come through. So, for that particular job Jacob was the choice he made for that and Esau was not. God chose the man to lead and the woman to help lead under the man's leadership.

On the same note it is not biblical for a man to mistreat a woman just because God made him the leader. He is responsible to GOD himself for how he treats his wife. The bible is VERY CLEAR on this message. A man is to love his wife as Christ loved the church and gave himself for it. There are men in offices of overseer ships all through this world who are not loving their wives as Christ loved the church. That my friend, you will have to answer to God for just as I had to for my former marriage.

Number eight, the deacon should be ruling his own house and children well. We discussed this in detail in the last chapter. The term children refer to the offspring of the person. The bible does not give a clear timeline as to when a child becomes an adult. But we do know that people were getting married at very young ages and having kids of their own. But however old we want to split these hairs on the father is to lead the child to God through love, discipline, and teaching him how to provide for his family. The only way a father can do this is through chasing God and setting that Godly example.

The bible tells us in I Tim. 3:13 that the man who has been appointed to the office of a deacon will purchase a good degree, and boldness in the faith which is only found in Christ Jesus. He will be a person who finds favor in God eyes. Anyone who walks with God will find favor in his eyes. This all comes back to one verse ***"But Seek ye first the Kingdom of God and hid righteousness and ALL THESE THINGS shall be added unto you" Matthew 6:33*** *(capitals* *added for emphasis)* we must be seeking God FIRST and not last. As a pastor, when you have men in your church who are chasing God and there is fruit of that, put them in the leadership roles so God can put his best on his church.

Now we can move onto question three "what is the responsibility of this office?" The main reference we have for a deacons responsibility is found in **Acts 6:1 And in those days, when the number of the disciples was multiplied, there arose a murmuring of the Grecians against the Hebrews, because their widows were neglected in the daily ministration.**

In this verse there were a group of people complaining to the apostles that some daily needs were not being met, and their widows were going every day without the things they needed. Then the apostles got the crowed together and told them that it was not going to be profitable for them (the twelve) to leave the preaching and teaching of the gospel and doctrines to attend to daily needs of the local assembly.

They told the crowd to pick out seven men with faith and of a good report, to appoint to the daily task and meet the needs of the widows. This does not mean that the church is required to meet all the needs of the widows. The widows are supposed to go to family first to get those needs met, then if there is no family then the church should step in. These seven men that were picked in verses 2-7 were ordained as deacons to assist in the daily physical needs of the congregation.

The bishops were to minister to the spiritual needs of teaching and discipling the individual, along with rebuking the gainsayers, while the deacon was to minister to the physical needs. In the modern-day church a deacon could maybe do maintenance work for someone in need, cut their grass, clean their car, or their wives could take a widow to the store to get groceries, a haircut or whatever the ministry need is. This is what we were mentioning earlier is why it was crucial for there to be no gossip as we get to learn people's personal lives.

The deacons are to be under the authority of the pastor as he is the one who appoints them. they are to be daily in prayer and seeking God. An office of a deacon is a two-person job as we see from the qualifications. It is the deacon himself and his wife. I at first wondered why the qualifications for a deacon also had qualifications for their wives, after studying Acts 6:1 it was because some of the deacon's duties was to minister to widows.

It is never good for a man to minister to a woman alone. This can lead to all kinds of temptation. We have heard many stories in our day where good men seeking God gave into these temptations and are no longer in the pulpit. Satan will use anything he can to tear down a man or woman of God. The bible speaks of abstaining from ALL the appearance of evil (I Thess. 5:22)

This does not mean that a married man talking to a single woman is a sin it simply says be smart about it. When I have to counsel with a woman, I tell them up front to go see my wife. If it is something I need to counsel with her about I tell that lady that my wife will be in the room with us. Worst case if I am approached with a distraught woman, I make sure we go outside to talk in plain view of others. This is the kind of practices that Pastors should do to abstain from that appearance. Give NO room to the devil, he will take an inch and stretch it ten miles and if the man is not focused on the word of God he will give into that temptation.

When a deacon goes to a widow's house or another woman's house to help, he needs to have his wife with him, if she is not available take another person but do NOT go alone. Since the deacon is responsible for the hands-on daily needs of the individual of the church his wife must be involved. As a team for Jesus they can accomplish what God has asked them to do through the pastor, every office of an overseer has one goal that is to edify the body of Christ.

The fourth and fifth questions for this office are a little easier to answer. We have already answered the fourth the question is: "Who was their ministry to" well their ministry is to the local church they have joined and been appointed to serve in. the fifth question is: "is this office still around in today's evangelical church?" the answer is yes.

As we discussed in the last chapter, the office of deacon is still around. However, in today's church this office has been combined with the some of the office of a bishop and then in actuality been elevated to the spiritual role instead of the physical role. I have not seen a church yet where the deacons do the daily physical ministration of the church. Churches today now have directors, or special committees, or whatever to handle these tasks.

 The deacons have become the spiritual leaders and, in some churches, have been allowed to be in an authoritative position. This is slippery ground when this happens, I would suggest proceeding with caution. However, at the end of the day it is the pastor's responsibility and God-given privilege to appoint any position to any task he desires to assist him in the church. The Pastor and only the Pastor is accountable to God directly and if that pastor is making decisions contrary to Gods plan, God will visit that upon that pastor.

Is it a sin to have a person in the role of a deacon who he or his wife does not meet the qualifications? I say no, that becomes the pastor's responsibility to make sure they are qualified. Is it a sin to only have deacons and not bishops? I say no. there is no mention in the bible of either being a sin. If a pastor puts people in positions that are not qualified or combines positions into one it can lead to stagnant spiritual growth. It on the other hand can work well if all the leadership is chasing God. If we draw nigh to God, he will draw nigh to us

8. Elders

Titus 1:5.....ordain elders in every city, ...

As we now go back down the road of Overseers, we come to the end of the road called Elder's way. Elders are mainly a people of an older age. When we look at the definition of an elder we find two consistent themes. ***In the New Testament Church the elders or presbyters***

were the same as bishops. It was an office derived from the Jewish usage of elders or rulers of the synagogues. And ***A person of greater age than someone specified.***" The term Elder is referring to the older more mature people of the time. This has led me to do some additional research, as I have been struggling to classify the Elders as an office of an overseer. There is no specific office listed in the bible as to what the elders do. So, we must, like the others use the consistencies of the bible to determine this title. For the sake of this study, to Rightly divide the Word of Truth, and against general opinion, I will not approach this as an office of an overseer.

An elder is a person who is basically a more mature person. This can work in the spiritual realm as well. Take for instance, you have an ordained elder in the church who may be in his forties, and then a man in his sixties comes in but is a new Christian, and just starting to grow in the Lord. The forty-year-old man has been growing in the Lord for a long time. The man in his forties would make a better elder than the man in his sixties because he has more maturity in spiritual growth.

In the New Testament church there are a couple of things we need to observe. First thing we see is that elders are always plural and not singular when they refer to ministering to the local church. They are appointed as a group setting. The second thing we must observe is they were separate of the priests. *Matthew 26:57-59 And they that had laid hold on Jesus led him away to Caiaphas the high priest, where the scribes and the elders were assembled. But Peter followed him afar off unto the high priest's palace, and went in, and sat with the servants, to see the end. Now the chief priests, and elders, and all the council, sought false witness against Jesus, to put him to death;* We see this in Matthew 26:57-59 they were identified separately. In many other bible passages as well, you will find the separate from the priest, scribes, and the leaders. The third thing to observe about the bible is it talks about the elders being ordained. This is where some of my struggle is to identify Elders as an office of an overseer. When Paul told Titus to ordain elders in every city, this was not to ordain as an office of an elder, but that the term elder is a general term meaning all those who have been ordained are the elders!

If a person has been ordained, he has the spiritual maturity, and growth to be an elder. I listed the definition from the dictionary where they compared them to a Bishop. In this comparison of them being a Bishop, the elders would be in the role of rebuking the gainsayers and helping to guide spiritually the individuals of the church not running the Pastor and the church. The term elder is and must be a general term to rightly divide the word of God. It is all through the bible. The elders could be an advisory group as well. A group of men with a lot of life experience to share to those younger or just starting out. We will see this in the chapters on Timothy, and Titus. There is nowhere in the bible where an elder has had charge of a church or group of people as an office of an overseer. For example, let's look at the founding of the United States. The United States had many men who got together and drafted the Declaration of independence, and the Constitution, these men today are called the elders of our nation.

The elders in most mainstream churches are used as the final authoritative body in the church. The Pastor works for the elders, and the elders work for the congregation. I heard a pastor on a radio program the other day say this was how his church operates. I have heard other pastors say they have to get with the elder board to make some of the decisions of the church. As we have seen in this study this is not how the bible has the local church set up.

If we go back to the chapter on Bishops we discussed that in other versions of the bible the word "bishop" had been changed to "Overseer" since overseer in itself is a general term as well than it paves the way for elders to be an authoritative board. Using the word "Bishop" as described in the King James Version it is NOT a general term but a specific office. This is where you must make the choice on which biblical world view you hold.

I will now refer to a quote from my son[5]. I love my son; he is an adult now on his own journey to seek God. He is in a church with an elder board rule. I was able to get a little feedback from him on his view of elders he wrote to me and said "if we look at all of the text then we can see that the qualifications are the same for a Pastor, Bishop, and Elder. That is because the idea of one man running a church was foreign to Paul and the churches of his day. Throughout church history we see that churches were ran by elders, some elders would hold the title

---

[5] J. Howe, used with permission

of Pastor (bishop) and others would not. However, all were held to the same standard. Churches were set up this way, to ensure that all men were held accountable. This lowered the risk of having one leader by himself preaching his own thing without any accountability"

In my sons statement the term elder is being identified as an office of an overseer. There is no evidence in the bible to support that this was an actual office. Elders are a combination of the offices of overseers. His quote also identified separate titles of elders, yet they are all the same as he stated above. As we have seen in this study the offices of overseers are NOT the same neither are the responsibilities the same. This is why God said in Ephesians 4:11 and he gave SOME, apostles, SOME prophets, SOME evangelists, SOME Pastors and teachers.

I am not against the idea of holding the leadership in the church accountable, that to me seems to be best practice. However, as we have discussed God himself holds the pastor accountable and will visit his sin upon him. And nowhere in the bible does it say that the leadership of the church works for the congregation of the church.

Now that we have shared both biblical world views of elders based on the elder being a specific office or a general term used for those in other offices who have been ordained, we can now move onto the five basic questions we ask of all the offices of overseers to determine which one it right.

The first question is "How is this office called, by God or appointed by man?" we see in Acts 14:23 and Titus 1:5 that elders were ordained in every city. Since they were ordained in Acts by the Apostles and by Titus in the book of Titus, we must answer the first question as they were appointed by man. In Acts 1:23 we see that after they were ordained then they were commended to the Lord. The Lord gave the apostles the freedom to appoint those who they felt were right for the job as God has granted Pastors with that also. This ordaining of elders as a general group of those in church leadership. And they did this in every church in every city. The elders are the ordained leadership of the church in general not a specific office.

The second question is "What are the qualifications of this office?" there are no qualifications for an office of an elder. Since there is no qualifications it cannot be an office it must be a general term for those in other offices of overseers I will go to *I Timothy 5:17 "Let the elders that rule well be counted worthy of double honour, especially they who labor in word and doctrine."* A Bishop is to labor in word and doctrine to rebuke the gainsayers.

Here we see a separation of the term elders. We see in this verse that the elders(plural) who rule well are to be counted worthy of double honor, ESPECIALLY those who labor in word and doctrine. Since it is identified that there are elders who labor in word and doctrine there are also those who don't. If the elders are an office on an overseer, then all elders would be to the same standard and this verse would not say "Especially they" singling out certain elders who are focused on word and doctrine. As we have already discussed in this book, those who labor in Word and Doctrine are the Pastors. The Bishops also need to labor in word and doctrine to fight against the untruth tellers. This is the whole reason why the other offices of overseers are even appointed so the that Pastor can feed his sheep with word and doctrine. The apostles appointed leaders so they could focus on the gospel, Paul told both Timothy and Titus to assist in appointing leadership in the churches to assist the pastors.

There are no qualifications for an elder in the bible, therefore it is not an office. If we go to biblical consistency, we see all other offices identified in some manner qualifications to be in that office, yet none are listed for an elder

The third question for the elders is "What is the responsibility of this office? There is no set responsibility in listed in the bible for the elders as an official office, except to oversee the church in their various assigned offices. We see this in Acts 20:17-28 where Paul is talking to ALL the elders in a general sense. In Verse 28 we see he tells them to "take heed" to themselves and all the flock, which the Holy Ghost had made them overseers.

The offices we have discussed in the previous chapters have had specific responsibilities in their individual office of an overseer. And all are elders of the local church, or in the bible. The bible is full of the term elder(s), it is mentioned 194 times in the bible, and all referring to an older person or persons with maturity and experience. In the next chapter on Timothy we will discuss the maturity of elders according to the bible.

We refer to I Peter 5:1-3, ***The elders which are among you I exhort, who am also an elder, and a witness of the suffering of Christ, and also a partaker of the glory that shall be revealed: Feed the flock of God which is among you, taking to the oversight thereof, not by constraint, but willingly; not for filthy lucre, but of a ready mind, Neither as being lords over God's heritage, but being ensamples to the flock.***

We see in this passage that Peter considered himself an elder. Peter was NOT part of the local church. He was not the pastor, or deacon, or bishop. However, he was an elder. This is a great biblical reference for showing that an elder is not an office of an overseer, but a general term. Peter was telling them to "Feed the Flock" all offices primary objective is to feed the flock whether in spiritual meeting of needs or in the physical meeting of needs. The last principal that Peter established was for them be ensamples. Ensamples is defined as examples. The elders are to feed the flock and set examples for the sheep to follow. They are not to be a governing board of the local church, that is the responsibility of the pastor.

The fourth question we must ask of the elders is "who was their ministry to?" well to put it as plainly as I can, their ministry was to the local people in the area where they were living, or in today's terminology, the local church where they are serving. Every time an elder or elders are mentioned in the bible, they are in the context of being people to go to who have exercised knowledge and wisdom from their life experiences.

If a church assigns an elder board it should only be an advisory board. A board of people who all through different life experiences can help give the pastor advice on certain matters. The pastor as a human being is not perfect, it is wise for him to seek godly council as needed. If an elder board is set up in this manner it would align with the principles of the bible. I challenge you to do your own study on elders in the bible.

Elders as a collective group of ordained men have their ministry centered on the ministry that either God has given them or that the pastor has appointed them to in the local church. In essence, their ministry is all over the world as the Lord leads them.
 The last question we will address for elders is:" is this office still around in today's evangelical

church?" the answer must be explained like this, first it is not an office, it is a general term. Then we must acknowledge both yes and no answers.

Let's take the yes answer for starters. Yes, in a lot of churches, and all modern-day, mainstream churches elder are used. They are used in a non-biblical way though. They are used as a governing board to which the pastor works for. We here in America have modernized and politicalized the church government structure. This has created an era of pride and haughtiness in the churches today. Just ask anyone in an elder position and watch them perk up, and smile and be proud of their "Position" in the church. They usher into church in their best attire, have their families act the perfect family role, most who have just been fighting with each other in the car on the way to church. This arrogance comes from being the authority in the church as an elder. They are special people who can solve all the churches problems. I say poppycock to all that.

If the church is set up the biblical way and the pastor and leadership is seeking God, I mean truly seeking God, this attitude will be severely reduced, and that person who has that kind of an attitude will be eventually replaced. If you think being a pastor is something that is all power and glory, I have news for you my friend it is not. When you think of the responsibility, and the accountability to God himself, it is very scary and overwhelming. A person cannot be walking with God and be walking with pride and arrogance at the same time.

Again, to the churches who have the elder board as a governing board and not as an advisory board, remember your pastor, not you, are accountable to God for that church. If the pastor tries to change the church to a biblical pastor led church and the board refuses than that pastor must turn it over to God and let him make those necessary changes. That pastor must do things Gods way without restrictions. I would encourage you to do a detailed study on Ezekiel 33:1-19 and see what happens when people do not heed the warnings God puts in place.

To the answer of NO, there are a few churches out there who do not use or recognize an elder board or even use the term elder in their churches. I grew up in an Independent, Fundamental bible believing Baptist church. Our church only had a Pastor and deacons, no elder titles. There is nothing wrong with only having deacons in the church serving under the Pastor.

The deacon position will be combined with the bishop position. If the church uses or does not use the term elder it makes no difference to God.

The only issue that arises is when we utilize the term elder as a governing board to rule the pastor and the church, who themselves then work for the church.

Why is it bad for elder board to work for the congregation? The congregation are the sheep. Who are not seeking God, who do not understand faith, and who quite honestly have their own agenda. The average church goer will cave into pressure from those that oppose what God is trying to do.

If the congregation gets members in who are not chasing God and they get to vote in or out their elders, then they in essence can control the pastor and what he preaches and teaches. the elders are afraid to lose the members or hurt their feelings, because they are the money givers in the church.

I can walk into any local Baptist church and on my very first visit to that church, at invitation time go down front and say I want to join the church, and I tell them yes I am saved, and have been baptized, and now I am a member. So now I can vote in meetings or vote on people being called for pastor or deacon or whatever. This has opened the door to allow evil into the midst of the church. it has been said that Satan is no longer fighting the church he is joining them. why, because Man has thought their system of church government is more important than what God has established in the bible. A Pastor-led church. how is evil coming into the church? by people joining and voting for people in eldership who themselves are not seeking God. The church body has a form of godliness but deny the power thereof. (II Timothy 3:5) if everyone is accountable to everyone else and no one is directly accountable to God, chaos will erupt. Do we need to discuss the evilness going on in the United Methodist church? they are getting ready to split on ordaining gay clergy to the pulpits. This is a horrible state that this denomination is in. but others are sure to follow. You watch, all, I repeat, all churches who are not accountable to God himself will eventually allow sin to be tolerated in their pulpits.

We have reduced the standard of accountability in the local church to a man-made non-perfect, sinful natured, board of elders and removed it from a perfect, non-sinful almighty God. This is a sad day and age. I must be honest, as I mentioned earlier my church is currently set up this way. Not reporting to a board of elders but in part working for the congregation. Our bylaws state that the church can vote out the pastor and vote him in. as I mentioned also over the next few months, we will be changing this to a one hundred percent pastor led church.

As we close out this chapter, we will see the biblical examples of a pastor led church and how these principles are practiced as we explore the duties of Timothy and Titus.

9. Timothy and Titus

I Timothy 1:2 "Unto Timothy, my own son in the faith: ......

As we have finished with the duties and responsibilities of the offices of overseers, we will now move the study to see how they are applied to the local church according to Timothy and Titus. Each of these two will have their own chapters in this study. We will still address the same five questions as we used in the offices of the overseers, to ensure the integrity of this study and the Word of God.

The first and most important thing we must determine is what office of an overseer was Timothy? Most people will say that Timothy was the pastor of the church here at Ephesus, I have read where some have compared him to the role of a bishop, in the local church. I cannot argue these opinions as there is no direct mention of which office he was assigned to.

I can say that by using biblical consistency, I am confident that Timothy was an evangelist and not the Pastor of the church. why do I say that, well we know that timothy traveled with Paul, II Corinthians 1:1, we know that he was appointed to stay at Ephesus to help get the false doctrines out of that church at Ephesus, I Timothy 1:18 and we read in II Timothy 4:5 that Paul told Timothy to "do the work of an evangelist, make full proof of thy ministry." And the church at Ephesus was already established, so it already had a Pastor. At the end of the book of II Timothy Paul calls for Timothy to return to him. A pastor does not leave his sheep he stays with them. So, all these fit the office of an evangelist.

Now to the first question: How was Timothy put into this office, was he called by God or appointed by man?" The answer to this question is Timothy was called of God as an evangelist. He traveled with Paul on his missionary journeys. Remember in the chapter on evangelists that evangelists were to go all over preaching the gospel, while missionaries are pastors who go to foreign lands and pastor churches. Both missionaries and evangelists had the title of evangelists.

Timothy is mentioned eight times in the bible, five of which are in the book of first and second timothy. The three other times that Timothy is mentioned is in II Corinthians 1:1, Hebrews 13:23, and Philemon 1:1. All three of these times Timothy is called the apostles' brother. He was in the gospel spreading ministry, as an evangelist he was able to travel and to stay at churches for a time as needed.

Since he was called by God as an evangelist, he had the gift of preaching and teaching. His call allowed him to be of an asset to the church at Ephesus which had been overrun with false doctrine. The bible does not mention why the false doctrine had gotten in the church to begin with. My personal conviction on this is that the bible was not written as we have it today and since the apostles were still around Jesus had recently risen from the dead. This church I believe was still in the establishment stage, and no guides were given at the time as to rebuke the false doctrines, except through the apostles and the churches they were planting. We today have the complete bible with all guidelines to life, and pastors have this guideline as well on how to run churches the biblical way.

Timothy was called by God to be an evangelist but was asked by Paul to stay at this church. the bible says in I Timothy 1:3 that Paul besought timothy to stay. Besought means to ask in a serious manner. Timothy was asked by Paul to stay and he chose to do so. This assignment was a temporary assignment as we will see in the end of II Timothy, where Paul asked for him to return back to him.

The second question we ask of Timothy was: "What were the qualifications of his office." We can read that answer in the chapter on evangelists. The basic qualifications are to obey Gods call, live by faith, and preach the gospel. The one qualification I need to remind you of is that evangelists did not pastor churches, they assisted for a short time as needed by the pastor of the local church.

The third question is: "What was Timothy's responsibility to his assignment?" we see that in the two books of the bible named after him, which we will discuss in brief detail. The first area of responsibility I want to start with is I Timothy 1:3 where Paul tells Timothy to "charge some" this means to entrust some of the leaders that they only teach bible doctrine and nothing else.

Since there was no completed bible at that time timothy had to teach them what he had learned. I believe the pastor of this church submitted to the wisdom of Paul as an elder and let Timothy come in and teach the elders of this church about the correct doctrine. As Timothy was to teach them what he had been taught he was entrusting them to teach that to the church congregation as well.

Timothy was to also tell the elders of this church not to listen to fables, and endless genealogies. All these no sensical questions can distract a leader from teaching the bible and it will create doubt to believer especially new ones. Timothy was to tell them to not give into them but to rather teach the church how to live godly lives and edify the body of Christ. Oh, how we need this in today's church.

It is very easy to get caught up in the folly of people who in all honesty have no desire to learn the word of God. These people will be people whose lives are bearing no fruit and are all chaos. They will ask questions according to their folly to not hear about the sin in their lives. I face this dealing with the unchurched. Our ministry is almost all unchurched people and they get very upset when the bible confronts their sin. My job as their pastor is not make them comfortable but to love them and to preach what the bible says without apology, or compromise.

Paul is expressing this in his letter to Timothy. We see this in verses four through eleven. Paul was giving this letter to Timothy as a guide on how to instruct this church in biblical doctrine. Timothy knew about the gospel of Jesus Christ and knew about biblical doctrine, since it was in writing it could be referred to as needed. Just as we have the bible today to refer to as often as needed for ourselves and our ministries

Paul, we see in chapter three was laying out the qualifications for the offices of bishops and deacons and talking about the women and their role in the church. the role of women in the church we addressed in the chapter of deacons and the requirements for their wives.

Paul is laying out in chapter four the guidelines for a minister of the gospel, not just a pastor, on how to walk in the way of the Lord. How you as a minister of the gospel walk in your daily life is crucial to the lost world. The lost world needs to see Jesus in us the hope of glory.

In chapters five and six of first Timothy Paul is telling timothy what the work of a minister of the gospel is to be about. The reason for timothy to have this is to help implement it in this local church. that was Timothy's responsibility on this assignment.
The next question we need to ask of timothy is: who was his ministry to?" first it was to wherever he went with Paul to preach and teach the word of God. For this particular instance he was to train the leadership at the church of Ephesus to follow the guidelines set by Paul under the inspiration of the Holy Spirit, in the books of first and second Timothy.

Timothy is a practical example of how to apply what God has given you to the ministry he has put you in. Timothy is a man to be studied and the books of Timothy are so full of knowledge about living a Christian life, and how to pastor a church. These books should be the first and foremost books that any bible student preparing for pastoring a church should know inside and out

The last question we will have to take a pass on, which is; "is this office still around today?" we know that the office of an evangelist is, but that Timothy is not.

We see in II Timothy chapter four verses 6-22 that Paul is summoning Timothy to return to him. He is giving him instructions to be diligent at returning as Paul knows he does not have much time left before he meets Jesus.

It was necessary to talk about Timothy for a bit, as the part of the controversy of the offices of an overseer is based on the requirements listed in I Timothy 3 and Titus 1.

I was initially going to do a chapter on Titus but the Holy Spirit is saying no. it is not crucial to this study. We can say the same thing about Titus that we have talked about with Timothy.

I will say there is stronger evidence that Titus was san Evangelist as well as Timothy according to chapter one verse five where Titus was told to ordain elders in EVERY city. Titus was at the church at Crete to educate them on biblical doctrines, and how to combat the false doctrines coming into this church. Then Titus was to go to other churches in the nearby cities as well to do the same there thus assisting the ushering in of the local church in every city.

There are many churches in every city. However not all are bible preaching churches. Make sure to support the bible believing, and bible preaching churches in your area

10. Priests

Hebrews 4:14 Seeing then that we have a great high
priest...Jesus the Son of God...

In this chapter we will need to discuss the role
that the priests played in the bible. I initially was
not going to put this in here as the role of a priest
is not really considered an "office" in the bible.

However, in commentaries, and bible dictionaries the priesthood is considered an office so we will address it.

We will need to look at the Old Testament priest then compare them to the New Testament priest as the Priesthood had changed. We must first understand the definitions for priest and priesthood.

A priest is simply defined as: a person who has the authority to lead or perform ceremonies in some religions and especially in some Christian religions….(Webster) the priesthood is defined as: "being a priest" (Webster) the "office" of the priest is considered the priesthood.

To get the best understanding of the Old verses the New testament priesthoods I want to encourage you to read Hebrews Chapters 4-10. We will focus on chapter seven verses 23-28.

Hebrews 7:23-28 And they truly were many priests, because they were not suffered to continue by reason of death: But this man, because he continueth ever, hath an unchangeable priesthood. Wherefore he is able also to save them to the uttermost that come unto God by him, seeing he ever liveth to make intercession for them. For such an high priest became us, who is holy, harmless, undefiled, separate from sinners, and made higher than the heavens; Who needeth not daily, as those high priests, to offer up sacrifice, first for his own sins, and then for the people's: for this he did once, when he offered up himself. For the law maketh men high priests which have infirmity; but the word of the oath, which was since the law, maketh the Son, who is consecrated for evermore.

The word priest in mentioned over 840 times in the bible. We hear this term today mostly used in the Catholic church. the priest is the one who forgives the sins of the people and leads them in the (mass) services which they have. As we look into the bible for what role a priest played, we will find that a priest being a sinful human being CANNOT forgive the sins of another sinful human being. Only God can forgive sins.

Priests sometimes were referred to in the same manner which an elder is referred to today. We see in Exodus 28:1 the word office is used in regards to Aaron, but this term office is referring to the priesthood itself.

There were many priests in the bible. The main ones we think of are Aaron and his sons. These were appointed by Moses through the direction of God himself. It is crucial that we understand the difference in the Old Testament priesthood and the priesthood in the New Testament. The reason we had to have priests in the old testament was to offer sacrifices for the sins of themselves and the people they were with.

Remember Jesus had not died on the cross at this time so there was no remission of sin. (Heb. 9:22). Sacrifices had to be made all the time. There were set days that the people would bring their sacrifices to the temple for the priests to offer up to God for the sins to be forgiven.

There is not enough time in this world to go verse by verse to show from the bible the sacrifices that were made for the people's sins. We also need to understand that in this time since Jesus had not yet come that the sins were merely coved and not removed.

No one could go to heaven except through Jesus. Once Jesus appeared on the scene then sins were removed. This is when God says what sins are you talking about? In the Old Testament the sacrifices had to be offered over and over again where in the New Testament Jesus had to be sacrificed only once for our sins.

I am referring to the above for the payment for sin as a whole. This payment is to replace the death that sin brings and allows a person to accept Christ as their Savior to go to Heaven. It is ONLY through the shed blood of Jesus that this is possible. We still today must ask forgiveness for the daily sins we commit and when our hearts get away from God. God is faithful to forgive our sins, and not only to forgive our sins but to cleans us from all wrongdoing. I John 1:9.

In the Old Testament sacrifices had to made for the daily sins as well. We see this in **Hebrews 7:26-27 For such an high priest became us, who is holy, harmless, undefiled, separate from sinners, and made higher than the heavens; who needeth not daily, as those high priests, to offer up sacrifice, first for his own sins, and then for the people's: for this he did once, when he offered up himself.**

We see that sacrifices had to be offered up daily. The high priests would have to offer up his sacrifice first before he could offer the sacrifice for the people. This "office" had no authority in leading any people to the Lord or feeding the sheep as has been described in other offices in this paper. It was simply for spiritual ceremony. The average person was not allowed into the temple to offer their own sacrifices and only the High Priest was allowed into the Holy of Holies. If anyone other than the ones God said to went into the temple they would be meet with death.

As we now discuss the New Testament priesthood it is simply this, we, the saved, Christians, Children of God, are the priest while Jesus is the High priest. Since Jesus was the sacrifice for our sins, the bible says we have a go-between between God and man. We can come to God ourselves, anytime, anywhere, in whatever condition we are in and talk to God and ask forgiveness for our sins.

A lost person must ask Jesus himself to come into his heart to be saved. I cannot, you cannot, your pastor cannot, ask Jesus to come into the heart of someone else, only they can.

Once Jesus has been asked into our hearts the Holy Spirit lives inside us and we have communication with God directly in the precious name of Jesus

I John 2:2 and he is the propitiation for our sins: and not for ours only, but also for the sins of the whole world.

The "he" in this verse is Jesus. Propitiation means an anointing sacrifice. Jesus did what only the priest could do in the Old Testament. The priests had to continually offer their sacrifices, while Jesus only had to offer his once.

The New Testament priesthood was changed upon the Death, burial and resurrection of our Lord and Savior Jesus Christ. It is a great thing, actually I would say it is a gift to be able to go to God on a whim and seek his forgiveness for ourselves. It builds a more intimate relationship with God. this allows the personal one on one relationship that God want us to have with him since before the world began.

Man originally had this one on one daily walk and talk with God in the Garden of Eden. Adam was able to see God and his face, and to literally walk with him, as Adam was created a perfect being. It was until Adam decided he was not satisfied with what God had given him and he ate of the fruit of the tree of the Knowledge of Good and Evil.

It excites my heart to know that because of the sacrifice of the Great High Priest (Jesus Christ) that we will have that daily personal walk with God again once the Lord returns to take his children home. We will be returned back to that perfect, sinless heavenly abode with God.

Romans 8:29 tells us that God knew us before we were born and that he predestinated us his children to be conformed to the image of Jesus. This means it was Gods intention in creating us, for us to be a sinless being so we could fellowship with him directly, face to face. Just as Jesus was a sinless being living here on the earth, we could have done that also. Once salvation is received, we are transformed back to the image of Jesus but not in the full manner it was intended. We will have the death payment for sin paid, but we with our sin natures will not be sinless even as Christians. Because of a non-sinless nature, we will not see the actual face of God until we reach Glory.

We are conformed back to this image through salvation to be children of God and Joint heirs with Jesus. What a glorious day that will be when my Jesus I shall see, when I look upon his face, the one who saved me by his grace.

We did not go with our typical five questions as there just was not enough time in this study to do that. But I challenge you to read and study the bible for yourselves. All I did was give a brief summary of priests as they were not really relevant for this study but needed to be mentioned.

11. Conclusion

Ephesians 4:12 " for the perfecting of the saints, for the work of the ministry, for the edifying of the body of Christ."

It has been my only desire in this study to "rightly divide the word of truth" I have learned more in this study than I could have ever imagined. I have experienced a deeper understanding of God grace than I had expected. I hope that you the reader will have made it a point to have approached this with the same mindset. If you approached this study with a one-way bias, you will truly have failed in understanding what the bible is truly saying.

This study is not written to any one person, or any denomination. It is not written to undermine any church government structure. It is simply to rightly divide the word of truth.

As we should always do with any study of the bible do not take this author's word for it simply based on what he says, verify it with the bible. Do this research for yourself and verify if the information in this study is correct.

I understand if you disagree with this, I will not get my feelings hurt, I had to write what the Lord placed on my heart. Let me leave you with this, are you truly ok with the little you get from God, or do you want everything you can get from God? if you want Gods all, you MUST give him your all, and run your ministries, whatever they may be, Gods way. Remember these five words: If I do, He will

You are loved

Matthew 6:33